Sensational Knitted SOCKS

Charlene Schurch

Martingale®
& COMPANY

Credits

President: Nancy J. Martin
CEO: Daniel J. Martin
VP and General Manager: Tom Wierzbicki
Publisher: Jane Hamada
Editorial Director: Mary V. Green
Managing Editor: Tina Cook
Technical Editor: Ursula Reikes
Copy Editor: Liz McGehee
Design Director: Stan Green
Illustrator: Robin Strobel
Cover and Text Designer: Regina Girard
Photographer: Brent Kane

Sensational Knitted Socks
© 2005 by Charlene Schurch

Martingale & Company
20205 144th Avenue NE
Woodinville, WA 98072-8478 USA
www.martingale-pub.com

Printed in China
10 09 08 07 06   8 7 6 5 4

Mission Statement

Dedicated to providing quality products and service to inspire creativity.

Library of Congress Cataloging-in-Publication Data
Schurch, Charlene.
   Sensational knitted socks / Charlene Schurch.
      p. cm.
   Includes bibliographical references.
   ISBN 1-56477-570-4
   1. Knitting—Patterns. 2. Socks. I. Title.
   TT825.S397 2005
   746.43'20432—dc22

                                                            2005014452

Dedication

To the long line of sock knitters who have produced so many wonderful knitting innovations to make sock knitting such a joy.

Acknowledgments

I wish to thank Beth Parrott for test knitting the original idea, knitting many of the alternative socks for the book, and providing a listening ear and good technical suggestions—there wouldn't be so many beautiful socks for you to see without her; Allison Judge for test knitting and continued encouragement; Candace Strick for encouragement and always believing I could figure it all out; and Rebecca Ewing for her colorful help.

I'd also like to thank Betsy Casey, Francine Rutter, Margery Winter, Molly Mahaffy, Mountain Colors, Trudy Van Stralen, and Therese Chynoweth for providing the wonderful yarns for the socks

And Fred, who, as always, makes it all possible.

CAMILLUS

Contents

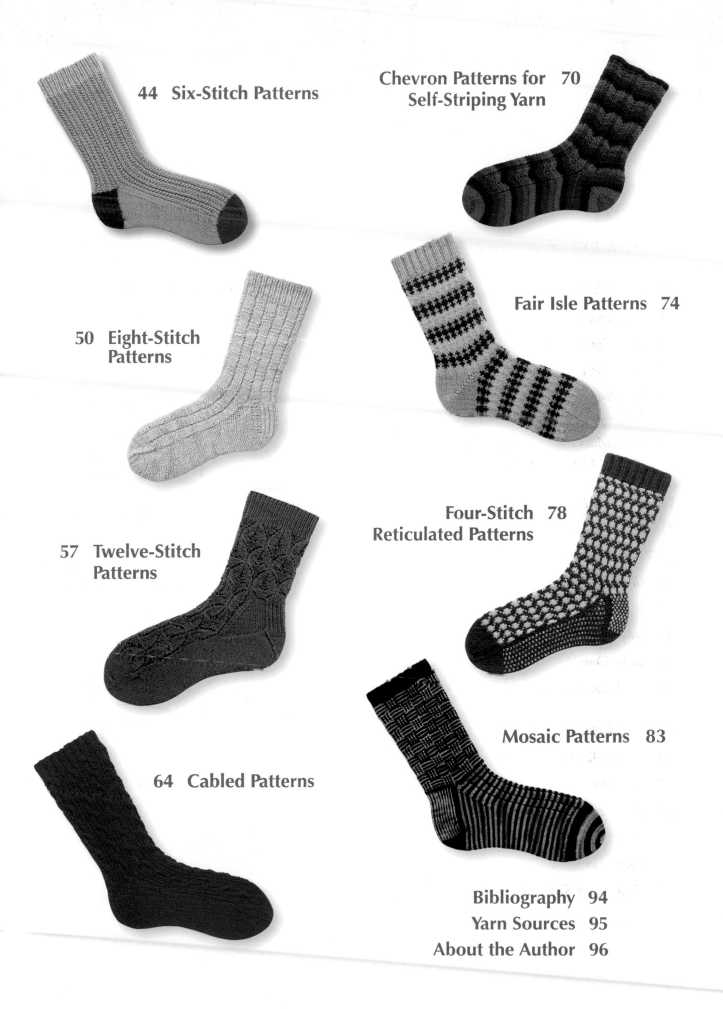

Preface

In my life, most of what I design is a reaction to something—a light kitchen evolved from the dark one we started with. The sock patterns here are a good example; they're a response to the fact that I am not "average" size—"one size fits all" doesn't work for me—and the fact that I can't work from a recipe without changing something.

While designing and knitting the socks, I had a hard time deciding on the exact pattern or structure—which design should I use on the heel or toe? Because it's possible to vary these elements, I worked to create a more flexible pattern structure to give you, the knitter, as many options as possible in creating socks that are truly yours. The choice of size, yarn, and pattern is all yours. For those of you who are more comfortable with specific instructions, I would encourage you to work with one pattern for a few pairs of socks. Then get courageous and change something: the pattern, the yarn, or the size. Knitting can be fun, creative, and uniquely your own.

Introduction

Socks are one of the most amazing knitted structures. As you knit, you're simultaneously creating fabric and a complex shape. Socks seem mysterious before you knit your first, but once you know it's possible, they're simple and fun. This book is a combination of basic information about knitting socks—yarn choices, technical skill requirements, and sizing information—and the master patterns for 10 different socks.

If you've never knit a sock before, I strongly recommend that you make the Class Sock to become familiar with the various sections of the sock and how they are worked. The patterns in this book include instructions for using three different needle techniques: four double-pointed needles, five double-pointed needles, and two circular needles. Making the Class Sock will allow you to try all three techniques on a small scale and decide which one you like best.

The projects are divided into 10 sock chapters, each of which is structured around the repeat of a pattern, for example, four-stitch patterns, six-stitch patterns, and so on. Each sock chapter contains a stitch dictionary with alternative patterns. You can happily knit for a long while from a single chapter—for different people, with different yarn, or in a new pattern—or you can try one chapter and then move on to other techniques. The sock chapters are arranged with the solid-colored socks first and color techniques following. All of the chapters are designed to provide maximum opportunities for you to customize your socks.

How to Use This Book

1. Read all of the information on pages 8–26.

2. Select the sock and then the stitch pattern you want to make.

3. Measure your foot or the recipient's foot. Or use the size charts on pages 13–14 to determine foot circumference.

4. In the project directions, refer to the stitch table for a range of appropriate gauges. Make sure the yarn you've selected will give you a satisfactory sock.

5. Choose the needles you're going to use for the sock, and then knit a gauge swatch.

6. Determine how many stitches to cast on by checking the stitch table as follows. Find your gauge in the leftmost column; then follow that row until you reach your foot circumference. If there's a number in the intersecting cell, that indicates how many stitches you should cast on. If the cell is blank, refer to "Stitch Tables" on page 15 to figure the number of cast-on stitches.

7. Familiarize yourself with the pattern. As you read through the directions, highlight the stitch counts for the size you're making. For example, there are 12 sizes in the Four-Stitch Ribbing Pattern sock on pages 33–38. If you're making the sock with a cast on of 64 stitches, which is the fifth number in the set of 12, you'll follow the stitch counts in the fifth position throughout the directions. You might want to photocopy the pattern for marking up.

8. Cast on and follow the directions in the appropriate column.

Sock Yarn

Wool is the best type of yarn for socks. I love wool because it makes a warm, cozy sock. Wool is elastic and absorbent, making it both easy to knit and comfortable to wear. Some manufacturers make 100% acrylic sock yarn, which is easy to wash and care for but not as comfortable to wear. Yarns with a high wool content that are labeled "sock" yarns tend to be most durable and may include some nylon or acrylic to make them wash and wear better. Cotton is added to some sock yarns for warm-weather wear.

Socks are probably laundered more often than other knitted items. I have found that machine washing my socks in cold water and air-drying them prevents shrinking and felting and makes them last longer. Be sure to check the washing instructions on the ball band (see "Yarn-Care Symbols" below).

Reinforcement Yarn

Reinforcement yarn is 75% Superwash wool and 25% nylon. Some sock yarns include a spool of reinforcement yarn that is dyed to match the sock yarn. This yarn is worked along with the sock yarn when working the heels and toes to make them more durable. If your sock yarn doesn't include a spool, you can purchase cards of reinforcement yarn separately at many yarn shops.

Yarn-Care Symbols

Below is a list of commonly used care symbols found on yarn labels. Be sure to pay attention to these and launder the socks as recommended.

Hand-Spun Yarn

As a hand spinner, I find it wonderfully satisfying to knit and wear socks made from my own hand-spun yarn. There are a few things to be aware of when choosing fiber to spin and when spinning to create durable, comfortable socks.

First you want a soft fiber. Be aware that merino or merino cross-sheep wool will be more likely to felt in the washing process. Merino is also a very soft fiber that wears out faster than some other coarser wools. If possible, blend the merino with some mohair for harder wear, more luster, and less felting.

The wool from Down sheep (these are typically sheep raised for meat production) make very good socks. The fiber is soft with great elasticity, has loft with a low luster, and has poor felting properties. Some better-known varieties of wool-producing sheep are Black Welsh Mountain, Cheviot, Clun Forest, Dorset Down, Hampshire Down, Montadale, Shetland, Suffolk, and Tunis. These breeds of wool are not as popular and may take some effort to find. Some other popular breeds that people use to knit socks include Polwarth, Rambouillet, Corriedale, Cormo, Targhee, Blue-Faced Leiceister, and Romney.

Spinning

There are many opinions about how to spin yarn for socks. I prefer to spin a medium-soft yarn and then knit with a relatively small needle to make a good, dense knitted fabric. Some prefer to knit a very tight

Washing

- Do not wash
- Hand wash in warm water
- Hand wash at stated temperature
- Machine wash
- Do not tumble dry
- Tumble drying OK
- Dry flat
- No bleach
- Chlorine bleach OK

Pressing

- Do not iron
- Cool iron
- Warm iron
- Hot iron

yarn for durability. Sometimes, however, the yarn can get so tight it's almost wiry, and this can be uncomfortable to walk on.

Washing Hand-Spun Socks

It is, of course, possible to wash your hand-spun socks in the sink with a little gentle detergent. I have been pleased with the results of machine washing them in cold water on gentle cycle and then air-drying. I find it best to be conservative when caring for something that takes so long to make.

Yarn Weights and Suggested Gauges

The ball band on many yarns gives a suggested needle size and target gauge. In my opinion, this gauge is often too loose for socks, which means there will be some drape to the fabric. But you don't want your socks to "drape"; you want a firmer, denser fabric. The advantage to knitting a tighter fabric for socks is that the fabric is more durable, which is important if you don't want to reknit or learn how to darn socks. It also makes the socks more comfortable. If the stitches are looser, they tend to dig into the bottom of your foot. When you knit tighter, a more uniform surface touches the foot. The downside of thicker fabric for socks is that it takes more yarn. This may mean that you have to purchase an extra ball of yarn for a large foot.

The following table lists four yarn weights with the recommended stitches over 1" of knitting and the suggested needle sizes for socks. Note that the gauge and needle size for socks is different from the standard gauge and needle size for sweaters knit from the same yarns.

Suggested Gauge and Needle Size		
Yarn Weight	Stitch Gauge per Inch	Needle Size
Fingering	8½ to 10 sts	U.S. 0 (2.0 mm) or 1 (2.25 mm)
Sport	7½ to 9 sts	U.S. 2 (2.5 mm)
DK	6½ to 8 sts	U.S. 3 (3.25 mm)
Worsted	6 to 7 sts	U.S. 4 (3.5 mm)

The following table indicates the approximate number of yards you can expect to find in 50-gram and 100-gram skeins or balls of yarn.

Yardage Yields		
Yarn Weight	Yards per 50 g	Yards per 100 g
Fingering	180 to 230	360 to 460
Sport	150 to 180	300 to 360
DK	120 to 145	240 to 290
Worsted	100 to 110	200 to 220

How Much Yarn Does It Take to Knit a Pair of Socks?

It depends—on the weight of the yarn, the size needles you're using, the size of the foot you're knitting for, and the density of the fabric you're creating.

Below is a chart of approximate yardage for socks knit with a single yarn. I have found that stranded knitting, as in Fair Isle patterning, can take up to 25% more yarn than knitting the same fabric with one yarn. Mosaic, slipped-stitch patterning is also denser than plain knitting, so you should consider buying more yarn when working these patterns. With experience, you'll begin to know how much yarn you need to buy. I suggest buying an additional ball of yarn; many yarn shops will take it back in trade, and then you'll avoid anxious hours wondering if you have enough yarn.

Approximate Yards Needed for a Pair of Socks				
Yarn Weight	Child (Small)	Child (Medium)	Women	Men
Fingering	275	340	430	525
Sport	215	275	370	430
DK	200	250	340	400
Worsted	185	215	310	370

Understanding sock construction and sock knitting techniques is important to your success in making them. This section covers the basics.

Sock Anatomy

To begin to understand how socks are constructed, pay attention to structure. If you're new to knitting socks, understanding sock structure may seem daunting. To make it easier, refer to the three examples that follow. I knit them using a different color for each section.

Top-down sock with heel flap

Top-Down Sock with Heel Flap

Cuff (gold): Generally, the cuff is worked in some kind of ribbing. This helps hold the sock up on the calf.

Leg (blueish green): This section is knit in your choice of pattern. It may be a continuation of the cuff pattern. Up to this point you're just knitting a tube.

Heel flap (reddish orange): Generally worked on 50% of the total sock stitches, the heel flap is knit back and forth. You need to make the tube of knitting turn 90° for the heel. Many heel flaps are worked in a heel-stitch pattern, which is a slip-stitch pattern that provides a denser piece of fabric where the sock receives a lot of wear. You can also make the heel flap more durable by knitting on smaller needles to create a denser fabric or by carrying reinforcement yarn along with the sock yarn.

Heel turn (violet): Also worked back and forth, this little triangle is knit using short rows, which means that you work part of the way across the heel flap, turn, and then work part of the way toward the other side. By working this way, you create the triangular shape that turns the direction of the knitting—quite remarkable for such a little bit of knitting.

Gusset and beginning of bottom of foot (yellow): Stitches are picked up and knit along the sides of the heel flap, and knitting resumes across the instep. At this point, there are more stitches than we started with, so decreases need to be worked to return to the original number of stitches.

Foot (dark green): The foot is worked even until the beginning of the toes.

Toe (red): Stitches are decreased on both sides of the sock, making the tube a little pointy so that it fits the toes and is comfortable in a pair of shoes.

Toe-Up Sock with Heel Flap

I prefer to knit my socks from the top down, but there are a couple of good reasons to work from the toe up. If you're concerned about having enough yarn for a pair of socks and you start at the toe, you will at least get the foot and heel completed. Then, if you determine that you'll run short of yarn, you can make the leg and cuff as long as the available yarn.

Some patterns are vertically symmetrical, and some are not. For example, from a slight distance you wouldn't know whether a simple rib had been worked from the top or the bottom of the knitting. More complex patterns may have a definite top and bottom. If you have a strong opinion about how a pattern should look, you may want to work that pattern from the toe up to preserve the up-and-down orientation of the pattern.

When working a heel-flap sock from the toe up, the heel flap is worked from the middle of the arch to the heel. This gives you the opportunity to reinforce the heel flap with nylon, work it in a heel stitch, or knit the heel flap with smaller needles—all ways to make that part of the sock stronger. This is an advantage when knitting socks for those who tend to wear out the bottom of their heels.

Toe (yellow): The toe is started with just a few stitches, and increases are evenly spaced until the correct number of stitches for the foot is reached.

Foot (blue): The foot is knit in a tube like any sock.

Heel flap (green): This portion is worked on 50% of the total stitches. The heel flap covers the wearer's heel and is structurally the same as the heel flap when working from the top down. It is knit in stockinette stitch. You could work the heel flap in the heel-stitch pattern with smaller needles or with reinforcement yarn to make it more durable if that is where you wear out your socks.

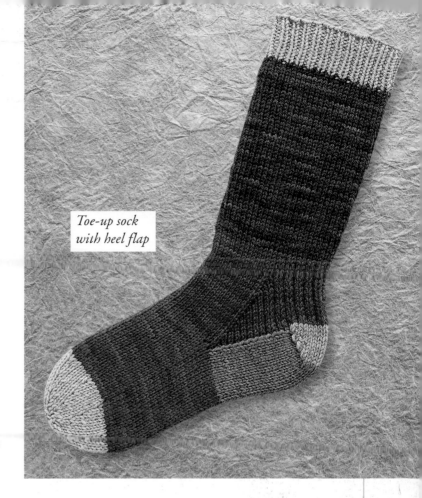

Toe-up sock with heel flap

Heel turn (gold): This little triangle creates the change of direction needed for an anatomical sock. Because it will be more at the bottom of the ankle than on the bottom of the foot as with the top-down version, you may want to start working in the heel-stitch pattern here if you tend to wear out your socks at this point.

Gusset and center-back heel (red): This portion of the sock covers the back of the heel and bottom of the ankle and is worked on the instep. You can work the center back portion that covers the heel in stockinette stitch or in the heel-stitch pattern for a more durable heel.

Leg (navy blue): This portion is worked in the round to the desired height.

Cuff (orange): The top part of the sock is worked in ribbing for some elasticity.

Top-down sock with short-row heel

Top-Down Sock with Short-Row Heel

Cuff (light green): This ribbing is worked in a different color and pattern from the leg to make an interesting-looking sock.

Leg (blueish green): The leg is worked in K2, P2 ribbing, a wonderfully elastic fabric that is easy to work and makes a great sock.

Stockinette band (yellow): In her socks, Priscilla Gibson Roberts knits a 1" stockinette band between the rib of the leg and the beginning of the heel. Commercial socks are made this way as well.

Short-row heel (violet): This heel is worked by knitting to one stitch short of the end of the row until about 20% of the stitches remain unworked. You then knit one more stitch on each row until you have knit all the stitches; you should have the same number of rows down to the heel as back to the foot.

Foot (orange): This foot is a tube of the same number of stitches as the leg. Notice that there is no gusset. This allows some design options for patterning that are easier than when working a sock with a heel flap.

Toe (blue and green): This is a standard toe. The blue part was knit with decreases every other round until there were half the number of stitches, and then the light green was knit with decreases every round

until there were about a quarter of the total number of stitches. Because the short-row heel is symmetrical, the structure of the sock is the same whether you knit from the top down or from the toe up.

Knitting Needles

You have many choices when selecting needles. It's important to try several kinds and make your own evaluations. I have heard some knitters extol the virtues of one style of needle, and after trying that style, I found that it did not suit me.

Several factors affect how comfortable needles are to knit with. The length of the needle varies on double-pointed needles and circular needles. If you're knitting a sock for a very large foot, the shorter double-pointed needles (4" or 5") may not be long enough to hold the stitches without accidentally dropping them off. Also, if you have large hands, the short needles may not be comfortable to hold. In these cases, choose the longer double-pointed needles. Short 16" circular needles have a shorter needle portion, which may also be uncomfortable, especially if you have large hands. Try 24" or longer needles because they have a longer needle portion that may be more comfortable to hold.

Knitting needles are made of a variety of materials that feel different in the hands. Plastic, nylon, wood, and bamboo tend to feel warmer than metal needles. Thinner needles, particularly plastic and some wooden ones, have a tendency to curve if you hold the needles tightly when knitting. Metal needles may feel cold in your hands and are more rigid.

Another important factor is the shape of the point. Wooden needles tend to have more rounded points, and some of the new plastic needles have very pointed tips. Not everyone likes the same style of needle. Try several and work with tools you enjoy.

Gauge Swatch

To get the most accurate gauge swatch, you should knit the swatch in the round using the pattern for the sock you want to make. But I have found that for all but the cable socks, you can knit a swatch back and forth in stockinette stitch to get a good idea of your gauge. Remember to wash and block the swatch before measuring it.

When working with a new yarn, I knit a flat swatch of at least 30 stitches and knit for about 4" in stockinette stitch. I try several different needle sizes to get a feel for the fabric I want for the sole of my foot. I then measure the portion of the stockinette-stitch fabric that I like the best to determine the gauge. It's a good idea to knit a few projects with the same-weight sock yarn so that you learn the gauge and density of fabric that you like to have for your socks. Then you'll begin to know about how many stitches are required for the socks you make. All of the gauge numbers refer to Stockinette stitch and accommodate the texture patterns of the socks.

I have often admired the socks knit with contrasting cuffs, heels, and toes. To determine how much yarn was required for each section, I knit a pair with different colors for the cuff, heel, and toe. I weighed the yarn before I started knitting and again when the socks were complete. The cuff, heel, and toe all take about the same amount of yarn. For the sock I made, about 21% of the total weight is in the cuff, heel, and toe (see the Twin Rib sock on page 44). The 21% is just an estimate; it all depends on the relative length of the foot and leg, but I was amazed to find that such a significant amount of yarn resides in those three areas.

The good news is that if you have some fun yarn left from a sock project, you may use it to knit the cuff, heel, and toe for a large sock or for one where you may run out of yarn. This is a far more attractive alternative than knitting the sock partway down the foot and then having to switch to a different yarn.

Foot Measurements and Sizes

It's helpful to know the foot circumference, the length of the foot, the length of the leg you want to knit, and the length of the heel. If the socks are for you, it's easy to measure your bare foot. If you cannot measure the recipient's foot, use the charts I have included for women, men, and children; they are based on shoe size.

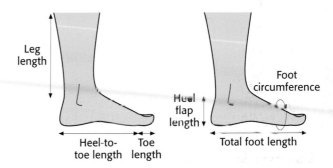

Size Chart for Women								
Shoe Size	Foot Circumference in Inches			Sock Length in Inches				
	Narrow	Medium	Wide	Leg	Heel Flap	Heel to Toe	Toe	Total Foot Length
5	6⅝	7½	8⅜	6⅛	2	7⅛	1⅝	8¾
5½	6¾	7⅝	8½	6¼	2	7¼	1⅝	8⅞
6	6⅞	7¾	8¾	6¼	2⅛	7¼	1¾	9
6½	7⅛	7⅞	8¾	6½	2⅛	7½	1¾	9¼
7	7¼	8⅛	9	6½	2¼	7⅝	1¾	9⅜
7½	7¼	8¼	9⅛	6¾	2¼	7¾	1¾	9½
8	7½	8⅜	9¼	6¾	2¼	8	1¾	9¾
8½	7⅝	8½	9⅜	6⅞	2¼	8	1¾	9¾
9	7¾	8¾	9½	7	2¼	8	2	10
9½	7⅞	8¾	9¾	7¼	2¼	8¼	2	10¼
10	8⅛	9	9¾	7¼	2¼	8¼	2	10¼
10½	8¼	9⅛	10	7⅜	2⅜	8½	2	10½
11	8⅜	9¼	10⅛	7⅝	2⅜	8¾	2	10¾
11½	8½	9⅜	10¼	7¾	2⅜	8¾	2	10¾
12	8¾	9½	10⅜	7⅞	2⅜	9	2	11

Size Chart for Men

Shoe Size	Foot Circumference in Inches			Sock Length in Inches				
	Narrow	Medium	Wide	Leg	Heel Flap	Heel to Toe	Toe	Total Foot Length
6	7¼	8¼	9⅛	6½	2⅛	7⅝	1¾	9⅜
6½	7½	8⅜	9¼	6¾	2⅛	7¾	1⅞	9⅝
7	7⅝	8½	9⅜	6¾	2¼	7¾	2	9¾
7½	7¾	8¾	9½	6⅞	2¼	7¾	2	9¾
8	7⅞	8¾	9¾	7	2¼	8	2	10
8½	8⅛	9	9¾	7⅛	2¼	8¼	2	10¼
9	8¼	9⅛	10	7¼	2¼	8¼	2	10¼
9½	8⅜	9¼	10⅛	7⅜	2⅜	8½	2⅛	10⅝
10	8½	9⅜	10¼	7½	2⅜	8⅝	2⅛	10¾
10½	8¾	9½	10⅜	7⅝	2⅜	8¾	2⅛	10⅞
11	8¾	9¾	10⅝	7¾	2½	8⅞	2⅛	11
11½	9	9¾	10¾	7¾	2½	8⅞	2¼	11⅛
12	9⅛	10	10⅞	7⅞	2⅝	8⅞	2⅜	11¼
12½	9¼	10⅛	11	8⅛	2⅝	9⅛	2⅜	11½
13	9¾	10¼	11¼	8¼	2⅝	9¼	2⅜	11⅝
13½	9½	10⅜	11¼	8¼	2¾	9⅜	2⅜	11¾
14	9¾	10⅝	11½	8⅜	2¾	9⅝	2⅜	12
14½	9¾	10¾	11⅝	8⅝	2¾	9¾	2⅜	12⅛
15	10	10⅞	11¾	8¾	2¾	9⅞	2⅜	12¼

Size Chart for Children

Shoe Size	Foot Circumference in Inches	Sock Length in Inches				
		Leg	Heel Flap	Heel to Toe	Toe	Total Foot
4	5	2⅞	1⅜	3⅜	⅞	4¼
5	5¼	3¼	1⅜	3½	1¼	4¾
6	5½	3¼	1¾	3¾	1¼	5
7	5¾	3⅝	1¾	4	1¼	5¼
8	6¼	3¾	1⅞	4¼	1¼	5½
9	6¼	4⅛	1⅞	4¾	1¼	6
10	6¾	4⅜	1⅞	4¾	1½	6¼
11	6¾	4¾	2	5⅛	1⅝	6¾
12	6¾	5	2	5⅜	1⅝	7
13	7	5¼	2	5¾	1⅝	7⅜

Stitch Tables

With a little help from lots of tables, you'll have the ability to knit socks in a wide range of sizes and yarns and in a variety of stitch-pattern repeats. The starting point for each sock is the stitch table, which tells you the number of stitches to cast on for your pattern. Let's look at the chart for the Four-Stitch Ribbing patterns.

Stitch Table															
	Foot Circumference in Inches														
Gauge Sts/1"	5	5½	6	6½	7	7½	8	8½	9	9½	10	10½	11	11½	12
	Number of Stitches to CO														
5½			32			40		48			56			64	64
6		32		40	40		48		56	56		64	64		72
6½	32					48		56		64	64		72	72	80
7			40		48		56		64		72	72		80	
7½		40		48		56		64		72		80	80	88	88
8	40		48		56		64		72		80		88		96
8½		48		56		64		72		80		88	96	96	104
9				64		72		80		88	96		104		
9½	48		56			72		80		88	96		104	112	112
10		56		64	72		80		88	96		104	112		120

The top row shows the circumference of the foot, which is the measurement taken with a tape measure around the widest part of the foot. The circumferences are in ½" increments. The column on the far left indicates the stitch gauges over 1", which are also in ½" increments. The body of the table gives you the number of required sock stitches. Notice that some cells are blank. You'll find out why below.

Let's take a hypothetical sock we want to knit. Our foot circumference is 8" and the gauge of our yarn is 8 stitches to the inch. Reading the chart, we see that we would cast on 64 stitches. If your foot circumference and/or your gauge are not exactly an even inch or half inch, multiply your foot circumference by your gauge, and then choose the number that is closest. For example, let's say we have an 8¼" foot circumference and a knitted gauge of 7¾". Multiplying the two, we get a result of 63.93. Rounding up to the nearest whole number tells us to use the 64-stitch sock.

What to do if you have a foot with an 8" circumference and a gauge of 7½"? If you look at the chart, the space is blank. If we do the math, we find that the result is 60. Well if 60 is divisible by 4, why is it not on the chart? Because 60 stitches would be 15 repeats of four stitches, which is an odd number of repeats. All the patterns are written so that half of the pattern stitches or repeats are knit on the instep of the sock. You have three options: you can knit the 56-stitch sock (14 repeats), which would be just about ½" smaller, knit the 64-stitch sock (16 repeats), which would be about ½" larger, or you can look in the other pattern sections for another 60-stitch sock. Once you've determined the number of stitches you'll use for your sock, circle or highlight all the numbers that apply to that number of stitches before you begin. This way, you can keep track of the proper instructions. For example, the Four-Stitch Ribbing patterns on pages 33–38 include 12 different cast-on numbers. Let's say you want to make the 64-stitch sock. Because the 64-stitch sock is the fifth position in the sequence of 12 numbers, you'll follow the numbers in the fifth position throughout the entire set of instructions.

More Durable Socks

One of the easiest ways to make a sock more durable is to knit with smaller needles at specific wear points. Each person walks in his or her own particular way and hence wears out the sock differently. It's simple to knit the heel flap with smaller needles for persons who wear out their heels. For the walker who wears out the bottom of the foot, changing to smaller needles when working the foot is one solution. Or, if you're using two circular needles, you may use a smaller one for the sole of the foot than for the instep; the difference in the row gauge will not show, and there will be a denser sole, which should wear out slower. There are several places where heavy wear is typical.

Heel: The heel rubs against the back of the shoe. Many sock patterns call for the heel to be worked in a "heel stitch," which is a slip-stitch pattern that produces a thicker and denser fabric. You can also use reinforcement yarn while knitting the heel to provide extra durability.

Heel flap: On a top-down sock, this is the part of the heel just beyond where the heel turn has been worked. Try changing to smaller needles for the heel flap to add durability. Or add a strand of reinforcement yarn while working the heel. If this does not solve the problem, you may want to try making a toe-up sock. At the point where you'll work the heel flap, you can switch to smaller needles, add a strand of reinforcement yarn, and work a heel stitch. You can continue with the smaller needles and the reinforcement yarn through the heel turn as well as working up the heel while doing the gusset decreases (see 12-stitch pattern on page 57).

Toes: Sometimes the big toe rubs against the sock. Again, you can add reinforcement thread to make the fabric stronger, or you can use smaller needles to make denser fabric. Or, you can do both.

Not Your Average Sock

Knitting socks for those whose feet are not average or for people with special needs can be challenging. Here are a few guidelines to help you with the most common issues.

Wide heels: Some people have thick heels, which makes it difficult to pull the sock over their heel. Or, if there is not enough fabric to go around the heel, the sock will sag, and eventually a good portion will be down in the shoe instead of around the ankle. The standard sock pattern is written using half of the stitches for the heel. Making the heel flap with 60% of the total sock stitches should alleviate this problem. Even though you have a sock with more stitches in the heel flap, it does not require more rows to be worked. For example, if the sock has 64 stitches, 60% of that is 38.4. I would look at the pattern and see how it centers and probably use 38 stitches for the heel flap. I would knit 32 heel-flap rows, which is standard for a 64-stitch sock. Using 38 stitches for the heel flap will leave 26 stitches for the instep. Work these stitches in the instep pattern. When you get to the toe, knit one round and rearrange the stitches so that there are 32 for the sole and 32 for the instep while working the toe.

Narrow heels: This is a person who has a narrow heel and a wider ball of the foot. It's best to use a fairly stretchy fabric that will accommodate the wideness at the toe, yet not bunch up in the foot, where it's narrower. It may also help to work the heel on 40% of the total stitches.

For example, if the sock has 64 stitches, use 26 sts for the heel and leave 38 on the instep. Again, you need to work 32 heel-flap rows so that the heel flap is long enough. When you're ready to work the toe, work one round in plain knit and rearrange the stitches for a normal toe.

High insteps: If the wearer finds the instep too tight on a sock, measure the person's heel and look at the length of the heel flap. It may be necessary to knit a few more rows of heel flap. This means you'll need to pick up more stitches for the gusset, and the gusset will be longer than on a standard sock. But that should be fine, because this foot needs more room in that area of the sock.

People who retain water or have thick ankles: You can knit the cuff and leg of the sock with a larger needle size so that there is no binding on the ankle. If the cast on is tight and uncomfortable, cast on twice the number of stitches needed for the sock by using the knitted cast-on method on page 22. Then in the first round, decrease the stitches around so that at the beginning of round 2 you have the proper number of stitches. For a 64-stitch sock, that would mean casting on 128 sts, and for a K2, P2 ribbing cuff, you would work the first round as follows: *K2tog, K2tog, P2tog, P2tog, rep from * around.

Pointy toes: It's possible to knit a pair of socks that have anatomically correct toes. It involves calculating separate decrease progressions on each side of the toe. While this has its charm, it requires that you wear a sock on its designated foot. I believe that socks wear longer if you randomly wear them on both feet, because the wear pattern is likely to be slightly different on each foot and you won't be wearing out the same place all the time. However, if a foot has pointy or long toes, take a look at the toe-decrease sequence. For the standard toe, the decreases are worked every other round until about half the stitches remain. Then the decreases are worked every round. If you need more room or want a pointier toe, continue to work the decreases every other round. Conversely, if your toes are short or the top of your foot is straight, start decreasing every round sooner than what is called for in the standard instructions.

Below are the basic techniques that are used for knitting the socks in this book.

Needle Techniques for Socks

All the patterns except the cable pattern include instructions for making socks with 3 different needle techniques: 4 double-pointed needles, 5 double-pointed needles, and 2 circular needles. The cable pattern includes directions for only 4 double-pointed needles and 2 circular needles. The 4 and 5 double-pointed needle techniques have been around for a long time. The 2 circular needles technique was popularized by Cat Bordhi (see "Bibliography" on page 94). The basics for casting on in each of the needle techniques are provided below.

Four Double-Pointed Needles

Cast on 100% of the stitches onto 1 of the double-pointed needles. Divide the stitches onto 3 double-pointed needles as follows:

Needle 1: 25% of stitches (begins with the first stitch you cast on)

Needle 2: 25% of stitches

Needle 3: 50% of stitches

Lay the needles on a flat surface and form a triangle so that needle 1 is on the left and needle 3 is on the right. The working end of the yarn should be attached to the last stitch on needle 3. Make sure that the stitches are not twisted. Use needle 4 to knit the stitches on needle 1. When you reach the end of those stitches, you'll have a free needle once again. Use this to knit the stitches on needle 2 and so on.

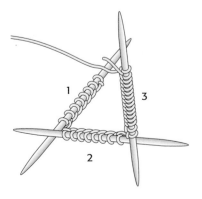

Five Double-Pointed Needles

Cast on 100% of the stitches onto 1 of the double-pointed needles. Divide the stitches onto 4 double-pointed needles so that each needle holds 25% of the stitches. Carefully lay the needles on a flat surface and form a rectangle so that needle 1 is on the left and needle 4 is on the right. The working end of the yarn should be attached to the last stitch on needle 4. Make sure that the stitches are not twisted. Use needle 5 to knit as described in "Four Double-Pointed Needles."

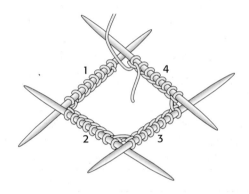

Two Circular Needles

Cast on 100% of the stitches onto 1 of the circular needles. Slip half the stitches to the second needle. Needle 1 holds the first stitches cast on and needle 2 holds the last stitches cast on and the working end of the yarn.

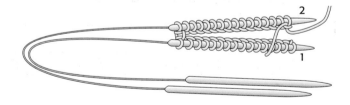

To start knitting on 2 circular needles, lay both needles on a flat surface with needle 1 closest to you and needle 2 (and working yarn) away from you. When you knit the stitches on needle 1, you'll use both ends of needle 1. Using the working yarn from needle 2, work the first stitch on needle 1 and pull the working yarn snug to close the gap between the 2 needles. Work the remaining stitches on needle 1. Rotate the work so that you're now ready to work the stitches on needle 2, using both ends of needle 2 to work those stitches. Continue working the cuff pattern around, first on needle 1 and then on needle 2. If you inadvertently use the end of needle 1 and the end of needle 2

(or vice versa), all the stitches will wind up on 1 of the needles. If this happens, just slip the stitches back onto the empty needle. Continue working in this manner until the cuff is the desired length. Switch to the leg pattern and continue until the leg is the desired length.

Working Socks

The following chart provides the basic structure for working socks in each of the 3 techniques. Instructions for each of the 3 techniques are provided in separate columns. Instructions that run across the whole chart apply to all 3 techniques.

Cuff and Leg		
CO 100% of sts and divide sts as directed above. Join and work cuff patt to desired length. Switch to leg patt and cont to desired leg length. If helpful, divide sts so that patt starts at beg of each needle; even if things are not symmetrical, it makes working far easier.		
Heel Flap		
Work heel flap back and forth on 50% of sts. Rearrange sts for heel, if necessary, so patt is centered over instep. For example, to center K2, P2 ribbing, move first and last sts of instep so end sts are P1. To do this, unknit last st and then:		
4 dpn	**5 dpn**	**2 circular needles**
Move 1 st from needle 3 to needle 1, 1 st from needle 1 to needle 2, and 1 st from needle 2 to needle 3. Heel is worked on sts on needle 3.	Move 1 st from needle 4 to needle 1, 1 st from needle 1 to needle 2, 1 st from needle 2 to needle 3, and 1 st from needle 3 to needle 4. Slip all sts from needle 4 to needle 3. Heel is worked on sts on needle 3.	Move 1 st from needle 2 to needle 1, and at other end, 1 st from needle 1 to needle 2. Heel is worked on sts on needle 2.
Heel flap is generally worked for same number of rows as sts in heel, unless otherwise instructed for special fit considerations.		
Heel Turn		
Work heel turn back and forth in rows, following directions as given for each sock.		

Gusset

Rearrange sts and renumber needles to work gusset and instep. PU sts for gusset (see page 25) as follows:

4 dpn	5 dpn	2 circular needles
Combine instep sts from needle 1 and 2 to just needle 2. Slip half heel turn sts to needle 1. Renumber needle with other half of heel turn sts to needle 4. (Needle 1 holds left half of sts when looking at RS of heel flap) Needle 1 (right side of foot): With half of heel sts on needle, PU 1 st for every 2 rows of heel flap, PU 2 sts at top of gusset. Needle 2 (instep): Work patt across instep. Needle 3 (left side of foot): PU 2 sts at top of gusset, PU 1 st for every 2 rows of heel flap, work rem half of heel sts from needle 4.	Slip half of heel turn sts to needle 5. Renumber needles so that sts of left half (while looking at RS of heel flap) are on needle 1 and those on right half are on needle 5. Needle 1 (right side of foot): With half of heel sts on needle, PU 1 st for every 2 rows of heel flap, PU 2 sts at top of gusset. Needles 2 and 3 (instep): Work patt across instep. Needle 4 (left side of foot): PU 2 sts at top of gusset, PU 1 st for every 2 rows of heel flap, work rem half of heel sts from needle 5.	Renumber needles: Needle 1 (heel): PU 1 st for every 2 rows of heel flap, PU 2 sts at top of gusset. PM, work half of instep sts. Needle 2 (instep): Work 2nd half of instep sts, PM, PU 2 sts at top of gusset, PU 1 st for every 2 rows of heel flap, knit half of heel flap sts from needle 1.

Sts per needle:

4 dpn	5 dpn	2 circular needles
Needle 1: Half of heel-flap sts plus sts picked up from side of heel flap Needle 2: 50% of original number of sts Needle 3: Half of heel-flap sts plus sts picked up from side of heel flap	Needle 1: Half of heel-flap sts plus sts picked up from side of heel flap Needle 2: 25% of original number of sts Needle 3: 25% of original number of sts Needle 4: Half of heel-flap sts plus sts picked up from side of heel flap	Needle 1: Half of heel-flap sts plus sts picked up from side of heel flap plus half of instep sts Needle 2: Half of instep sts, plus sts picked up from heel flap and other half of heel-flap sts

Gusset Decrease

Beg of rnd is now the bottom center of the foot.
Work rnd 1 once to combine sts picked up and to eliminate gap at top of gusset.

Rnd 1	Rnd 1	Rnd 1
Needle 1: Knit to last 2 sts, ssk. Needle 2: Work patt across instep. Needle 3: K2tog, knit to end.	Needle 1: Knit to last 2 sts, ssk. Needles 2 and 3: Work patt across instep. Needle 4: K2tog, knit to end.	Needle 1: Knit to 2 sts before marker, ssk, SM, work patt across instep. Needle 2: Work patt across instep sts to last st before marker, P1, SM, K2tog, knit to end.

Rnd 2 Needle 1: Knit to last 3 sts, K2tog, K1. Needle 2: Work patt across instep. Needle 3: K1, ssk, knit to end.	**Rnd 2** Needle 1: Knit to last 3 sts, K2tog, K1. Needles 2 and 3: Work patt across instep. Needle 4: K1, ssk, knit to end.	**Rnd 2** Needle 1: Knit to 3 sts before marker, K2tog, K1, SM, work patt to end. Needle 2: Work patt to marker, SM, K1, ssk, knit to end.

Rnd 3: Work patt as established.

Rep rnds 2 and 3 until you're back to original number of CO sts. Transfer sts as necessary to return to original st placement.

Needle 1: 25% Needle 2: 50% Needle 3: 25%	25% of sts on each needle	50% of sts on each needle. Transfer all the instep sts to needle 1 and the sole sts to needle 2 and put away your markers.

Note: If you wind up with an unequal number of sts on 1 side or the other of the heel flap, just work 1 more dec rnd at the end to even things out. It will not show.

Foot

Cont in St st on sole and in patt on instep until you reach desired heel-to-toe length.

Toe Shaping

4 dpn	5 dpn	2 circular needles
Knit sts on needle 1. Beg of rnd now shifts to side of foot that is ready to work instep. Needle 1: 50% sts (instep) Needle 2: 25% sts (sole) Needle 3: 25% sts (sole)	Knit sts on needle 1. Beg of rnd now shifts to side of foot that is ready to work instep. Needle 1: 25% sts (instep) Needle 2: 25% sts (instep) Needle 3: 25% sts (sole) Needle 4: 25% sts (sole)	Needle 1: 50% sts (instep) Needle 2: 50% sts (sole)

Work dec as follows:

Rnd 1	Rnd 1	Rnd 1
Needle 1: K1, ssk, knit to last 3 sts, K2tog, K1. Needle 2: K1, ssk, knit to end. Needle 3: Knit to last 3 sts, K2tog, K1.	Needle 1: K1, ssk, knit to end. Needle 2: Knit to last 3 sts, K2tog, K1. Needle 3: K1, ssk, knit to end. Needle 4: Knit to last 3 sts, K2tog, K1.	Needle 1: K1, ssk, knit to last 3 sts, K2tog, K1. Needle 2: K1, ssk, knit to last 3 sts, K2tog, K1.

Rnd 2: Knit around.

Rep rnds 1 and 2 as instructed in pattern.

Rep rnd 1 only as instructed in pattern.

Place sts from top of sock on 1 needle and sts from bottom onto 2nd needle. Graft toe sts tog with kitchener st (see page 24).

Cast On

Three different cast-on methods are used for the socks in this book.

Long-Tail Cast On

The long-tail cast on is elastic and sturdy. Use this technique when casting on for a sock that begins with ribbing.

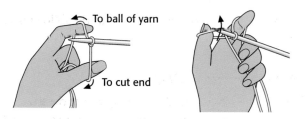

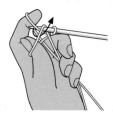

To work the long-tail cast on, make a slipknot with a tail about 4 times the length of the sock circumference. Or, starting at the end of the yarn, wrap the yarn around the needle the same number of times as the stitches you're casting on; make the slipknot there. The tail is the free end, and the long end is the yarn attached to the ball. Place the slipknot on the right-hand needle. Hold both lengths of yarn in the left hand, the tail over the thumb, and the long end over the index finger. Both ends are tensioned by holding them in the palm with the other fingers. Insert the right-hand needle into the front of the loop on the thumb and over the yarn on the index finger. Bring this yarn through the loop on the thumb, forming a loop on the needle; tighten gently by placing the thumb under the yarn now coming from the needle and gently pulling back on it. This same motion sets up the loop on the thumb for the next stitch. Repeat this operation for the required number of stitches.

Provisional Cast On

This technique is used when casting on for a toe-up sock. It's also used when you need to pick up stitches from the cast on so that you can knit in the opposite direction. This cast on provides very little bulk so that after you pick up and knit in the opposite direction, the join is undetectable. The waste yarn is easiest to take out after the stitches have been picked up.

Work with waste yarn and a double-pointed needle in your left hand, and a crochet hook with a slipknot in your right hand. Place the double-pointed needle over the long strand held in your left hand. With the hook, draw a loop over the needle and through the slipknot. Place the yarn under the needle again, *with the hook, draw a loop over the needle and through the stitch on the hook, rep from * until you have one stitch less than the number required. Transfer the last loop from the crochet hook to the needle after you have moved the yarn to the back of the needle. Cut the waste yarn and begin knitting with sock yarn.

Crochet a chain over top of knitting needle.

To remove the chain, unravel the crochet chain, placing each stitch on the needle.

Knitted Cast On

This is a very loose and insubstantial cast on. It's best used when you're going to cast on twice the number of stitches needed and work the first row as *knit 2 stitches together* across to yield the correct number for your sock. This is also a wonderful cast on if you're knitting a hem. The little loops of the cast on are easy to pick up and you can then knit or sew the hem in place. The hem does not bind, nor is it too tight.

To work the knitted cast on, make a slipknot and place it on the left-hand needle. Insert the right-hand needle into the loop and knit a stitch; place the new stitch on the left-hand needle. I like to place the new stitch on the left-hand needle as if to knit, which means that both needles are in the loop with the points up. If you work in this manner, you can just tighten up on the stitch and start working the next stitch. You now have 2 stitches on the left-hand needle. Knit into the next stitch on the left-hand needle and place the third stitch on the right-hand needle.

Continue in this manner until you have the number of stitches you need.

Knit into stitch.

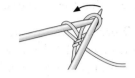
Place new stitch on left needle.

Decreases

When knitting a gusset, the decreases are paired along the sides of the foot. You'll use different decrease methods for the left and right sides of the foot.

Right-Slanting Decrease

I recommend just one method (knit 2 together) for the right-slanting decrease because it yields such beautiful results.

Knit two together (K2tog): This decrease is typically used on the left-hand side of the knitted fabric. Knit 2 stitches together through the front loops as 1 stitch. The decreased stitches will line up beautifully.

Left-Slanting Decrease

This decrease is typically used on the right-hand side of the knitted fabric. There are a number of ways that knitters can make this decrease, although none of them look as beautiful as the *knit 2 stitches together* when they are worked. After the knitting is washed, they all look better, but still not as nice as the *knit 2 stitches together*. In the text, I have indicated *slip, slip, knit* for a left-leaning decrease. You may substitute any of the other decreases; however, I would advise that you choose one and stick with it for consistency in the look of the sock.

Slip, slip, knit (ssk): Slip the first and second stitches, one at a time, as if to knit, then insert the point of the left-hand needle into the fronts of these 2 stitches, and knit them together from this position. Because knitters are always looking for better ways to do things, you may want to try slipping the first stitch as if to knit and the second one as if to purl. Some knitters find they like the appearance of this method better.

Slip one, knit one, pass slipped stitch over (sl 1, K1, psso): Slip 1 stitch as if to purl with the yarn in back, knit the next stitch, and then pass the slipped stitch over the knit stitch and off the needle.

Knit two together through the back loop: Knit 2 stitches together through the back loops as 1 stitch.

Increases

There are many ways to increase, but the following are 2 ways used in this book.

Make One Stitch (M1)

With the left-hand needle, pick up the horizontal strand between the last stitch and the next stitch, and knit it through the back of the loop.

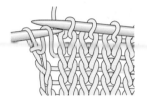 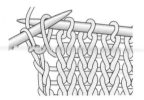

Knit One into Front and Back (K1f&b)

Knit into the front and back of the same stitch. You have 1 more stitch on the needle.

Heel-Flap Selvages

The patterns are written with either a chain selvage or a garter selvage. My favorite way to work a chain selvage is to knit the first stitch of each heel-flap row and slip the last stitch as if to purl with the yarn in front. The advantage to this is that you're slipping the edge stitch and working it immediately following. This leaves less opportunity for that stitch to loosen. If it's a little loose, you can tighten up when working the first 2 stitches of the heel flap. The garter selvage is worked by knitting the first stitch on WS rows and the last stitch on RS rows, and then purling the last stitch on WS rows and the first stitch on RS rows.

Picking Up into a Chain Selvage

You have the choice of picking up both loops of the chain or just the outside loop of the chain. The fabric of the heel flap wants to curl under, so you need to unroll it to make sure you can see the whole selvage edge when you're working.

Picking up both loops of chain: Insert the needle under both loops of the chain and pick up a new stitch. This produces a neat edge and leaves the chain on the inside of the sock.

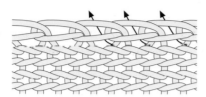

Pick up both loops of chain.

Picking up outside loop of chain: This creates a twisted, more decorative stitch and leaves the inside of the sock the smoothest. Use a spare needle to pick up the outside loop and knit it through the back of the loop.

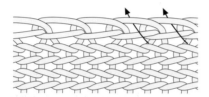

Pick up outside loop of chain
to create twisted stitch.

Picking Up into a Garter Selvage

This is perhaps the easiest way to work a heel flap and gusset. Pick up the thread between the garter bumps. You'll be starting at a garter bump at the heel and begin with the thread above the bump.

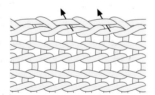

Pick up thread between
garter beads.

Grafting or Kitchener Stitch

Use this technique to sew the ends of the toes together. Work with the 2 pieces on the needles with wrong sides together, 1 needle behind the other. Thread a tapestry needle with the yarn attached to the back needle and work as follows:

- Insert the tapestry needle into the first stitch of the front needle as if to purl, and pull the yarn through but leave the stitch on the knitting needle. Go to the back needle, being careful to take the yarn under the knitting needle each time. Insert the tapestry needle into the first stitch as if to knit, and pull the yarn through but leave the stitch on the knitting needle.

- *Insert the tapestry needle into the first stitch of the front needle as if to knit, and then slip this stitch off the needle. Insert the tapestry needle into the next stitch of the front needle as if to purl, and pull the yarn through but leave the stitch on the knitting needle.

- Go to the back needle and insert the tapestry needle into the first stitch as if to purl. Take this stitch off and onto the tapestry needle. Put the tapestry needle through the next stitch of the back needle as if to knit, and pull the yarn through but leave this stitch on the knitting needle.*

- Repeat from * to * until all stitches are joined. Don't draw the yarn too tightly. The stitches should have the same tension as the knitted stitches. Fasten the end securely.

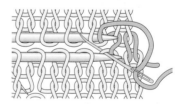

Here's a shorthand way of remembering how the grafting is done:

Front needle: *Knit off, purl on.*

Back needle: *Purl off, knit on.*

You can avoid the problems that often plague sock knitting by using a few simple techniques. Also included in this section are tips for reading the charts in this book.

Avoiding Ears on Heel Turn

As careful as I was about picking up stitches for the gusset, I sometimes noticed a little "ear" at one side of the heel turn. In thinking about the way most socks are knit, I realized there is 1 extra row worked after the heel is turned. If you're working with heavier yarn, this extra row accounts for the ear. So I tried completing the heel turn on a right-side row, eliminating the need to work a plain knit row before picking up gusset stitches. I eliminated the ear! This way of working is not standard, and for those of you who reflexively knit that way, pay attention to the instructions. All the heel flaps start on a wrong-side row, because you turn first, not after the first row has been worked.

Avoiding Gap at Top of Gusset

The hole or gap at the top of the gusset is a perennial problem for sock knitters. Some instructions don't provide any suggestion for how to alleviate this situation, and some suggest picking up 1 stitch, without any specifics on exactly where or how to do this.

I like to pick up 2 extra stitches at the top of the gusset. The way to identify these stitches is to look for the horizontal thread between the first instep stitch and the heel-flap stitch. Insert the needle into the left half of the heel-flap stitch and pick up 1 stitch; then pick up the right half of the first instep stitch from the row below the stitch on the needle. Both of these stitches are on the gusset needle.

When picking up the gusset on the other side of the sock, again locate the horizontal thread between the instep and heel flap; pick up the outside halves of each stitch and place on the needle to be used for the heel gusset. If these stitches have been purled, just pick

up through the purl bump. These 2 extra stitches are worked together on the first gusset round.

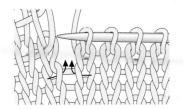

Picking up stitches when both were knit

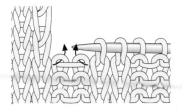

Picking up stitches when both were purled

Reading Stitch Counts in Pattern Charts

As you look through the instructions for the various sock patterns, you'll see the phrase "sts per needles" followed by a series of numbers in parentheses.

When you see several sets of parentheses, the numbers within each set of parentheses relates to a specific sock size. When you see a single number, followed by a set of numbers in parentheses, it means that each number relates to a specific sock size, and those stitches are divided evenly over the number of needles in that technique.

For example, in the 5-dpn method, if the stitch numbers are divided unevenly over 4 needles, you will see something like this: "(15, 8, 8, 15), (18, 10, 10, 18)." The first set of numbers, (15, 8, 8, 15), are the stitches on needles 1, 2, 3, and 4 for the 32-stitch cast on. The second set, (18, 10, 10, 18), are the stitches on needles 1, 2, 3, and 4 for the 40-stitch cast on, and so on for each different cast-on number.

However, if the stitches are divided evenly over all 4 needles, you will see a single number outside a set of parentheses followed by a series of numbers within the parentheses, for example, 8 (10, 12, 14, etc.). The first number, "8," outside the parentheses is for the 32-stitch cast on and means that there will be 8 stitches on each of the 4 needles. The next number, "10," inside the parentheses is for the 40-stitch cast on and means that there will be 10 stitches on each of the 4 needles and so on for each different cast-on number.

Reading Stitch-Dictionary Charts

The charts for the stitch patterns represent what the knitting looks like from the right side or outside of the work and are for working the patterns in the round only. All charts are read from right to left for every row and from bottom to top. For example, work the first round by knitting the stitches in the chart from right to left and repeat that sequence until you have completed the first round. Then move to the second row of the chart and begin working those stitches, also from right to left, until that round is complete.

The written instructions for the patterns are also intended for knitting in the round so that you may follow the text if you're more comfortable with that format.

Editing the Width of Patterns

If you have yarn that you love and a particular pattern selected, but alas, it's not a multiple that will work for your size, all is not lost. Think about editing the stitch pattern by adding an additional purl stitch or deleting one. Try the math to see if this gets you closer to a number of stitches that will fit you.

Abbreviations and Glossary

approx	approximately
beg	begin(ning)
BO	bind off
cn	cable needle
CO	cast on
cont	continue
dec	decrease(ing)
dpn	double-pointed needle(s)
EOR	every other row
est	established
g	gram(s)
inc	increase(ing)
K	knit
K1-b	knit 1 stitch through back loop
K1f&b	knit into front and back of same stitch
K2tog	knit 2 stitches together (see page 23)
K3tog	knit 3 stitches together
kwise	knitwise
LH	left hand
M1	make 1 stitch (see page 23)
MC	main color
P	purl
patt(s)	pattern(s)
PM	place marker
psso	pass slipped stitch over
p2sso	pass 2 slipped stitches together over
P2tog	purl 2 stitches together
P3tog	purl 3 stitches together
PU	pick up and knit
pwise	purlwise
rem	remain(ing)
rep	repeat(s)
RH	right hand
rnd(s)	round(s)
RS	right side
sl	slip
sl st	slip stitch purlwise with yarn in back unless otherwise noted
SM	slip marker
ssk	slip, slip, knit (see page 23)
st(s)	stitch(es)
St st	stockinette stitch
tog	together
TW2R	knit 2 stitches together and leave stitch on left-hand needle, knit first stitch and slip both stitches off needle together
wyib	with yarn in back
wyif	with yarn in front
WS	wrong side
yb	yarn back
yds	yards
yf	yarn forward
YO	yarn over

Skill Levels

◨☐☐◨	Beginning
◨■☐◨	Easy
◨■■◨	Intermediate
◨■■■	Experienced

Symbol Key for Charts

☐ K

⊟ P

▨ TW2R

⬚⁵ Work 5 sts (K1, YO, K1, YO, K1) into next 2 sts tog

◺ ssk

◹ K2tog

⊡ YO

▪ No stitch

◭ sl 1, K2tog, psso

⋁ K1, P1, K1 in front of next st

▭◁ Sl 1, K2, psso the 2 knit sts

◹ K3tog

2 Knit into front and then back of the YO

⋔ P3tog, knit same 3 sts tog, P same 3 sts tog again, and slip all 3 from needle

◹• P3tog

⊟ sl 1 wyib

⋀ sl 1 wyif

◹• P2tog

◺ sl 2, K1, p2sso: insert needle into next 2 sts on left needle as if to K2tog, and slip them to right needle, knit next st, then pass 2 slipped sts tog over knit st

▾ K1, YO, K1 in 1 st

⅄ K1-b

⧅ sl 2 sts to cn hold in back, K2, K2 from cn

⧅ sl 2 sts to cn, hold in front, K2, K2 from cn

⧅ sl 3 sts to cn, hold in front, K3, K3 from cn

Class Sock

This is the sock I teach in my beginning sock classes. It's written for 32 stitches and includes instructions for three different needle techniques: four double-pointed needles, five double-pointed needles, and two circular needles. If you want to learn a new needle technique, I recommend that you knit this little sock so that you become comfortable with the technique before embarking on a whole pair of socks. Refer to pages 18–21 for more information on these techniques.

Materials

1 skein of worsted-weight yarn—white or natural is ideal. Working with a smooth, unvariegated, light-colored yarn makes it easy to see what's happening with your knitting.

1 set of size 6 needles for desired needle method

Coilless safety pin (optional)

Ring markers (for 2 circular needles technique)

Cuff and Leg

Using long-tail CO method, CO 32 sts. Divide sts per needle as follows:

4 dpn	5 dpn	2 circular needles
8, 8, 16	8, 8, 8, 8	16, 16

Join, being careful not to twist sts (if you twist the sts at this point, you'll have a twist in the tube and an unwearable sock). Pay attention to this spot because it's beg of rnd; use tail left over from CO as visual reminder of the place to start patt rnds. You can also use a coilless safety pin to indicate beg of rnd.

Work K2, P2 ribbing for 3". Notice that sts are divided so that you can work patt starting with K2 at beg of each needle. *I find that dividing the sts so patt begins at beg of each needle, even if things are not symmetrical, makes working far easier.*

Heel Flap

The heel is worked on half of the total sts (16). Because ribbing cont on 16 instep sts, it will look better to center patt on instep. If sts are left as is, patt on instep would start with K2 and end with P2. To center ribbing, we want first and last sts of instep to be P1. To do this, unknit last st and then:

4 dpn	5 dpn	2 circular needles
Move the unknit purled st from needle 3 to needle 1, then move 1 st from needle 1 to needle 2, 1 st from needle 2 to needle 3. Heel is worked on sts on needle 3.	Move the unknit purled st from needle 4 to needle 1, 1 st from needle 1 to needle 2, 1 st from needle 2 to needle 3, and 1 st from needle 3 to needle 4. Combine sts on needles 3 and 4 tog. Set needle 4 aside for now. Heel is worked on sts on needle 3.	Move the unknit purled st from needle 2 to needle 1, and at other end, 1 st from needle 1 to needle 2. Heel is worked on sts on needle 2.

Beg to work heel st on WS row. Yes, you must turn work around and start knitting on a WS row.

Row 1 (WS): K1, purl to last st, sl last st as if to purl with yarn in front (sl 1, wyif).

Row 2: K1, *sl 1 wyib, k1, rep from * to last st, sl 1 wyif.

Rep rows 1 and 2 until you have 16 total rows of heel flap, ending with row 2. An easy way to make sure you're on track is to count slipped sts on heel flap. Because they are worked every other row, there will be 8 of them.

Heel Turn

Row 1 (WS): Sl 1, P8, P2tog, P1, turn.

Row 2: Sl 1, K3, ssk, K1, turn.

Note that there will be a small gap between the working sts that form the heel turn and the unworked heel sts. The P2tog and ssk that you'll be working will close the gap.

Row 3: Sl 1, P4, P2tog, P1, turn.

Row 4: Sl 1, K5, ssk, K1, turn.

Row 5: Sl 1, P6, P2tog, P1, turn.

Row 6: Sl 1, K7, ssk, K1—10 heel-flap sts rem.

Notice that when you're working short rows, you're working 1 more st between the gap each time.

Rearrange sts and renumber needles as follows:

Combine instep sts from needles 1 and 2 to just needle 2. Slip half heel turn sts to needle 1. Renumber needle with other half of heel turn sts to needle 4.	Slip half the heel turn sts to needle 1. Renumber needle with other half of heel turn sts to needle 5.	Needle 1: Heel sts Needle 2: Instep sts

Gusset		
4 dpn	**5 dpn**	**2 circular needles**
Needle 1: PU 8 sts from side of heel flap, PU 2 sts at top of gusset (see page 25). Needle 2: P1, *K2, P2, rep from * to last st, P1. Needle 3: PU 2 sts at top of gusset, PU 8 sts from side of heel flap, knit rem heel sts.	Needle 1: PU 8 sts from side of heel flap, PU 2 sts at top of gusset (see page 25). Needle 2: P1, *K2, P2, rep from * to last st, P1. Needle 3: P1, *K2, P2, rep from * to last st, P1. Needle 4: PU 2 sts at top of gusset, PU 8 sts from side of heel flap, knit rem heel sts.	Needle 1: PU 8 sts from side of heel flap, PU 2 sts at top of gusset (see page 25), PM, P1, K2, P2, K2, P1. Needle 2: P1, K2, P2, K2, P1, PM, PU 2 extra sts at top of gusset, PU 8 sts from side of heel flap, K5 heel sts from needle 1. Each needle now has half of instep sts and half of sole sts.

Sts per needle:

15, 16, 15	15, 8, 8, 15	23, 23

Gusset Decrease		

Beg of rnd is now center sole of foot.
Work rnd 1 once to combine sts picked up and to eliminate gap at top of gusset.

Rnd 1 Needle 1: Knit to last 2 sts, ssk. Needle 2: P1, *K2, P2, rep from * to last st, P1. Needle 3: K2tog, knit to end.	**Rnd 1** Needle 1: Knit to last 2 sts, ssk. Needle 2: P1, *K2, P2, rep from * to last st, P1. Needle 3: P1, *K2, P2, rep from * to last st, P1. Needle 4: K2tog, knit to end.	**Rnd 1** Needle 1: Knit to 2 sts before marker, ssk, SM, P1, *K2, P2, rep from * to last st, P1. Needle 2: P1, *K2, P2, rep from * to last st before marker, P1, SM, K2tog, knit to end.
Rnd 2 Needle 1: Knit to last 3 sts, K2tog, K1. Needle 2: Work est patt across instep. Needle 3: K1, ssk, knit to end.	**Rnd 2** Needle 1: Knit to last 3 sts, K2tog, K1. Needles 2 and 3: Work est patt across instep. Needle 4: K1, ssk, knit to end.	**Rnd 2** Needle 1: Knit to 3 sts before marker, K2tog, K1, SM, work patt to end. Needle 2: Work patt to marker, SM, K1, ssk, knit to end.

Rnd 3: Work est patt.
Rep rnds 2 and 3 until 32 total sts rem. Transfer sts as necessary until you return to original st placement:

8, 16, 8	8 sts on each needle	16 sts on each needle Rearrange sts so that all instep sts are on needle 1 and all sole sts are on needle 2.

Note: If you wind up with an unequal number of sts on one side or other of the heel flap, just work 1 more dec rnd at the end to even things out. It will not show.

Foot		

Cont St st on sole and centered K2, P2 ribbing on instep until foot measures 3" from beg of heel flap.

Toe Shaping		
4 dpn	5 dpn	2 circular needles
Knit sts on needle 1. Renumber needles: Needle 1: 16 instep sts Needle 2: 8 sole sts Needle 3: 8 sole sts	Knit sts on needle 1. Renumber needles : Needle 1: 8 instep sts Needle 2: 8 instep sts Needle 3: 8 sole sts Needle 4: 8 sole sts	Needle 1: 16 instep sts Needle 2: 16 sole sts
Work dec as follows:		
Rnd 1 Needle 1: K1, ssk, knit to last 3 sts, K2tog, K1. Needle 2: K1, ssk, knit to end. Needle 3: Knit to last 3 sts, K2tog, K1.	**Rnd 1** Needle 1: K1, ssk, knit to end. Needle 2: Knit to last 3 sts, K2tog, K1. Needle 3: K1, ssk, knit to end. Needle 4: Knit to last 3 sts, K2tog, K1.	**Rnd 1** Needle 1: K1, ssk, knit to last 3 sts, K2tog, K1. Needle 2: K1, ssk, knit to last 3 sts, K2tog, K1.

Rnd 2: Knit around.

Rep rnds 1 and 2 until 16 total sts rem.

Rep rnd 1 only until 12 total sts rem.

Place sts from top of sock on 1 needle and sts from bottom onto 2nd needle. Graft toe sts tog with kitchener st (see page 24).

Congratulations! You've completed the Class Sock and have graduated to being a sock knitter. Now that you have worked through the sock structure with perhaps a new needle technique, you are ready to select the size, yarn, and pattern for your next sock.

Things to Remember

Slipping stitches: For all patterns in this book, slip all stitches purlwise unless instructed otherwise.

Beginning-of-round marker: I use the tail left over from the cast on as a visual reminder that this is the spot for the beginning of the round. You may also use a coilless safety pin to mark this spot.

Picking up gusset stitches along heel flap: Refer to page 23 for picking up stitches on chain selvages or garter selvages.

Eliminating the gusset gap: To eliminate the gap at the top of the gusset, pick up 2 extra stitches in the row below where you're working as follows: 1 stitch is from the left half of the purl stitch that became the heel flap and the other stitch is the right half of the first instep stitch. Both of these stitches will be on the gusset needle (see page 25).

Last rows of heel turn: When working the last 2 decrease rows of the heel turn, you may end with a decrease; there will be no additional stitch to knit or purl. This is not an error.

Symbol key for charts: The key to the charts is on page 28. But you can look at the written instructions for the pattern if you are unsure what a symbol means.

If you get lost along the way: Refer to the appropriate section in the front of this book to get back on track.

Four-Stitch Ribbing Patterns

Many basic sock patterns are written for *knit 2, purl 2* ribbing, which is wonderfully elastic and functional. With a little modification, knitters have created many beautiful variations. You may choose from several that have *knit 2, purl 2* for the first round and then vary a bit on subsequent rounds to create a more interesting fabric and a more pleasurable knitting experience.

Materials

Referring to "Sock Yarn" and "Sock Basics" on pages 8–17, gather materials for the socks you'd like to make.

Ring markers (for 2 circular needles technique)

Garter Rib made with Weaver's Wool Quarters from Mountain Colors (color Rimrock) on size 3 (3.25 mm) needles with a gauge of 7½ sts to 1".

Baby Cable Rib made with Plus Cotton Color from Regia (color 57) on size 2 (2.75 mm) needles with gauge of 7½ sts to 1".

Elongated Corded Rib made with Gems Opal from Louet Sales (color 57 French Blue) on size 3 (3.25 mm) needles with gauge of 7 sts to 1".

33

Directions

Select the number of sts to CO based on the gauge for your yarn and needles and the circumference of the intended foot.

Stitch Table															
Gauge Sts/1"	**Foot Circumference in Inches**														
	5	5½	6	6½	7	7½	8	8½	9	9½	10	10½	11	11½	12
	Number of Stitches to CO														
5½			32		40			(48)			56			64	64
6		32		40	40		48		56	56		64	64		72
6½	32				48		56			64	64		72	72	80
7		40		48		56			64		72	72		80	
7½		40		48		56		64		72		80	80	88	88
8	40		48		56		64		72		80		88		96
8½		48		56		64		72		80		88	96	96	104
9					64	72		80			88	96		104	
9½	48		56			72		80		88	96		104	112	112
10		56		64	72		80		88	96		104	112		120

Cuff and Leg

Using long-tail CO method, CO 32 (40, 48, 56, 64, 72, 80, 88, 96, 104, 112, 120) sts.
Divide sts per needle as follows:

4 dpn	5 dpn	2 circular needles
(8, 8, 16), (10, 10, 20), (12, 12, 24), (14, 14, 28), (16, 16, 32), (18, 18, 36), (20, 20, 40), (22, 22, 44), (24, 24, 48), (26, 26, 52), (28, 28, 56), (30, 30, 60)	8 (10, 12, 14, 16, 18, 20, 22, 24, 26, 28, 30)	16 (20, 24, 28, 32, 36, 40, 44, 48, 52, 56, 60)

Join, being careful not to twist sts, and work K2, P2 ribbing for 1½". Then change to patt of choice. Work to desired leg length, ending with completed last row of patt rep and ready to work Rnd 1; this is essential to work the heel properly.

Heel Flap

The heel is worked back and forth in rows on 16 (20, 24, 28, 32, 36, 40, 44, 48, 52, 56, 60) sts beg with WS row and ending with RS row.

Rearrange sts to center patt over instep. Unknit last purl st of rnd and then:

Move unknit purled st from needle 3 to needle 1, then move 1 st from needle 1 to needle 2, and 1 st from needle 2 to needle 3. Needle 1: Instep sts Needle 2: Instep sts Needle 3: Heel sts	Move unknit purled st from needle 4 to needle 1, 1 st from needle 1 to needle 2, 1 st from needle 2 to needle 3, 1 st from needle 3 to needle 4. Sl all the sts from needle 4 to needle 3. Needle 1: Instep sts Needle 2: Instep sts Needle 3: Heel sts	Move unknit purled st from needle 2 to needle 1, and at the other end 1 st from needle 1 to needle 2. Needle 1: Instep sts Needle 2: Heel sts

Work in heel st with 3-st garter border. Starting with a WS row, TURN work before first row.

Row 1 (WS): K3, purl to end.

Row 2: P3, *K1, sl 1, rep from * to last 3 sts, K3.

Rep rows 1 and 2 until you have 16 (20, 24, 28, 32, 36, 40, 44, 48, 52, 56, 60) total rows in heel flap.

Heel Turn

Work as follows:

Row 1 (WS): Sl 1, P8 (10, 12, 14, 16, 18, 20, 22, 24, 26, 28, 30), P2tog, P1, turn.

Row 2: Sl 1, K3, ssk, K1, turn.

Note that there will be a small gap between working sts that form heel turn and unworked heel sts.

Row 3: Sl 1, purl to within 1 st of gap, P2tog, P1, turn.

Row 4: Sl 1, knit to within 1 st of gap, ssk, K1, turn.

Rep rows 3 and 4, inc 1 additional knit or purl st after the sl 1 until all side sts are worked, end with completed row 4. There should be 10 (12, 14, 16, 18, 20, 22, 24, 26, 28, 30, 32) sts left on heel flap.

Note that for ease of instructions, beg of rnd is now at center of bottom of foot. The needles are renumbered at this point. Needle 1 is beg of rnd.

Gusset

4 dpn	5 dpn	2 circular needles
Divide heel sts evenly onto needles 1 and 4. Sts on needles 1 and 4: 5 (6, 7, 8, 9, 10, 11, 12, 13, 14, 15, 16) sts. Needle 2: instep sts, then:	Divide heel sts evenly onto needles 1 and 3. Sts on needles 1 and 5: 5 (6, 7, 8, 9, 10, 11, 12, 13, 14, 15, 16) sts. Needles 2 and 3: instep sts, then:	Needle 1: Heel sts Needle 2: Instep sts With RS of work facing you and needle 1, cont as follows:
PU 8 (10, 12, 14, 16, 18, 20, 22, 24, 26, 28, 30) sts from side of heel flap, PU 2 sts at top of gusset (see page 25).		
Needle 2: Work across instep in patt. Needle 3: PU 2 sts at top of gusset, PU 8 (10, 12, 14, 16, 18, 20, 22, 24, 26, 28, 30) sts from side of heel flap, knit rem heel sts. Sts per needle: (15, 16, 15), (18, 20, 18), (21, 24, 21), (24, 28, 24), (27, 32, 27), (30, 36, 30), (33, 40, 33), (36, 44, 36), (39, 48, 39), (42, 52, 42), (45, 56, 45), (48, 60, 48)	Needles 2 and 3: Work across instep in patt. Needle 4: PU 2 sts at top of gusset, PU 8 (10, 12, 14, 16, 18, 20, 22, 24, 26, 28, 30) sts from side of heel flap, knit rem heel sts. Sts per needle: (15, 8, 8, 15), (18, 10, 10, 18), (21, 12, 12, 21), (24, 14, 14, 24), (27, 16, 16, 27), (30, 18, 18, 30), (33, 20, 20, 33), (36, 22, 22, 26), (39, 24, 24, 39), (42, 26, 26, 42), (45, 28, 28, 45), (48, 30, 30, 48)	PM, work half of instep sts in patt. Needle 2: Work half of instep sts in patt, PM, PU 2 sts at top of gusset, PU 8 (10, 12, 14, 16, 18, 20, 22, 24, 26 28, 30) sts from side of heel flap, knit half of heel-flap sts from needle 1 to needle 2. *The needles hold left half and right half of foot sts rather than sts for instep and bottom of foot.* Sts per needle: 23 (28, 33, 38, 43, 48, 53, 58, 63, 68, 73, 78)

Gusset Decrease

Work rnd 1 once to combine sts picked up and to eliminate gap at top of gusset.

Rnd 1	Rnd 1	Rnd 1
Needle 1: Knit to last 2 sts, ssk. Needle 2: Work est patt. Needle 3: K2tog, knit to end.	Needle 1: Knit to last 2 sts, ssk. Needles 2 and 3: Work est patt. Needle 4: K2tog, knit to end.	Needle 1: Knit to 2 sts before marker, ssk, SM, work est patt to end. Needle 2: Work est patt to marker, SM, K2tog, knit to end.

Rnd 2 Needle 1: Knit to last 3 sts, K2tog, K1. Needle 2: Work est patt. Needle 3: K1, ssk, knit to end.	**Rnd 2** Needle 1: Knit to last 3 sts, K2tog, K1. Needles 2 and 3: Work est patt. Needle 4: K1, ssk, knit to end.	**Rnd 2** Needle 1: Knit to 3 sts before marker, K2tog, K1, SM, work est patt. Needle 2: Work est patt to marker, SM, K1, ssk, knit to end.

Rnd 3: Work est patt.

Rep rnds 2 and 3 until 32 (40, 48, 56, 64, 72, 80, 88, 96, 104, 112, 120) total sts rem.

Foot

4 dpn	5 dpn	2 circular needles
Cont St st on needles 1 and 3, and est patt on needle 2 to desired heel-to-toe length.	Cont St st on needles 1 and 4, and est patt on needles 2 and 3 to desired heel-to-toe length.	Rearrange sts so instep sts are on needle 1, and sole sts are on needle 2. Markers are no longer needed. Cont est patt to desired heel-to-toe length.

Toe Shaping

Adjust beg of rnd to side of foot as follows:

Knit sts on needle 1. Needle 1: Instep sts Needle 2: Half of sole sts Needle 3: Half of sole sts Sts per needle: (16, 8, 8), (20, 10, 10), (24, 12, 12), (28, 14, 14), (32, 16, 16), (36, 18, 18), (40, 20, 20), (44, 22, 22), (48, 24, 24), (52, 26, 26), (56, 28, 28), (60, 30, 30)	Knit sts on needle 1. Needle 1: Half of instep sts Needle 2: Half of instep sts Needle 3: Half of sole sts Needle 4: Half of sole sts Sts per needle: 8 (10, 12, 14, 16, 18, 20, 22, 24, 26, 28, 30)	Knit to marker. Needle 1: Instep sts Needle 2: Sole sts Sts per needle: 16 (20, 24, 28, 32, 36, 40, 44, 48, 52, 56, 60)

Work dec as follows:

Rnd 1 Needle 1: K1, ssk, knit to last 3 sts, K2tog, K1. Needle 2: K1, ssk, knit to end. Needle 3: Knit to last 3 sts, K2tog, K1.	**Rnd 1** Needle 1: K1, ssk, knit to end. Needle 2: Knit to last 3 sts, K2tog, K1. Needle 3: K1, ssk, knit to end. Needle 4: Knit to last 3 sts, K2tog, K1.	**Rnd 1** Needle 1: K1, ssk, knit to last 3 sts, K2tog, K1. Needle 2: K1, ssk, knit to last 3 sts, K2tog, K1.

Rnd 2: Knit around.

Rep rnds 1 and 2 until 16 (20, 24, 28, 32, 36, 40, 44, 48, 52, 56, 60) total sts rem.

Rep rnd 1 only until 8 (12, 12, 16, 16, 20, 20, 24, 24, 28, 28, 32) total sts rem.

Place sts from top of sock on 1 needle and sts from bottom onto 2nd needle. Graft toe sts tog with kitchener st (see page 24).

Stitch Dictionary

Instructions are for working patterns in the round. All rows of charts are worked from right to left and from bottom to top.

Garter Rib

Rnd 1: *K2, P2, rep from *.
Rnd 2: Knit.
Rep rnds 1 and 2.

Baby Cable Rib

Rnds 1, 2, 3: *K2, P2, rep from *.
Rnd 4: *K2tog and leave sts on needle, knit first st and slide both off needle, P2, rep from *.
Rep rnds 1–4.

Elongated Corded Rib

Rnds 1, 2: *K2, P2, rep from *.
Rnd 3: *Ssk, YO, P2, rep from *.
Rnds 4, 5, 6: *K2, P2, rep from *.
Rnd 7: *YO, K2tog, P2, rep from *.
Rnd 8: *K2, P2, rep from *.

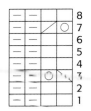

Double Moss

Rnds 1, 2: *K2, P2, rep from *.
Rnds 3, 4: *P2, K2, rep from *.
Rep rnds 1–4.

Openwork Rib

Rnds 1, 2, 3: *K2, P2, rep from *.
Rnd 4: *YO, ssk, P2, rep from *.
Rep rnds 1–4.

Crossover Rib

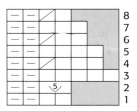

Rnd 1: *K2, P2, rep from *.
Rnd 2: *Work 5 sts (K1, YO, K1, YO, K1) into next 2 sts tog (treat the 2 sts tog as 1 st when working the 5 sts), P2, rep from *.
Rnd 3: *K5, P2, rep from *.
Rnd 4: *K3, K2tog, P2, rep from *.
Rnd 5: *K4, P2, rep from *.
Rnd 6: *K2, K2tog, P2, rep from *.
Rnd 7: *K3, P2, rep from *.
Rnd 8: *K1, K2tog, P2, rep from *.
Rep rnds 1–8.

Waffle Rib

Rnds 1, 2, 3: *K2, P2, rep from *
Rnd 4: Purl.
Rep rnds 1–4.

Alternating 2 x 2 Rib

Rnds 1, 2, 3, 4: *K2, P2, rep from *.
Rnd 5: *TW2R, P2, rep from *.
Rnds 6, 7, 8, 9, 10: *P2, K2, rep from *.
Rnd 11: *P2, TW2R, rep from *.
Rnd 12: *K2, P2, rep from *.
Rep rnds 1–12.

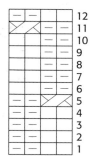

Corded Rib

Rnd 1: *K2, P2, rep from *.
Rnd 2: *Ssk, YO, P2, rep from *.
Rnd 3: *K2, P2, rep from *.
Rnd 4: *YO, K2tog, P2, rep from *.
Rep rnds 1–4.

Woven Stitch

Rnds 1, 2: *K2, P2, rep from *.
Rnds 3, 4: Knit.
Rnds 5, 6: *P2, K2, rep from *.
Rnds 7, 8: Knit.
Rep rnds 1–8.

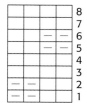

Purled Ladder

Rnd 1: *K2, P2, rep from *.
Rnd 2: Knit.
Rnd 3: Purl.
Rnds 4, 5: *P2, K2, rep from *.
Rnd 6: Knit.
Rnd 7: Purl.
Rnd 8: *K2, P2, rep from *.
Rep rnds 1–8.

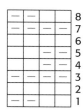

Waffle Rib II

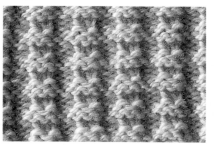

Rnds 1, 2: *K2, P2, rep from *.
Rnds 3, 4: Purl.
Rep rnds 1–4.

Four-Stitch Ribbing Patterns

Five-Stitch Patterns

The basic structure of the patterns in this section is a combination of 2 purl stitches with 3 knit or patterned stitches. It's amazing what adding 1 stitch will do to the complexity of the patterns. The socks are worked from the toe up in short rows. This method creates a cup or pocket around your toes.

Materials

Referring to "Sock Yarn" and "Sock Basics" on pages 8–17, gather materials for the socks you'd like to make.

Small amount of waste yarn for provisional CO

Skill Level: Easy ◼◼◻◻

Yarn over Cable made with Lang JaWoll from Berroco (color 175 Peach) on size 1 (2.25 mm) needles with a gauge of 9½ sts to 1". This sock is made with Short Row Toe.

Beaded Rib made with Kid Mohair and Polwarth Wool from Rovings (color 13 Raspberry) on size 3 (3.25 mm) needles with a gauge of 6 sts to 1".

Laburnum made with Kroy Socks 4 Ply from Patons (color 54733 Grass Green) on size 2 (2.75 mm) needles with a gauge of 8½ sts to 1".

These socks were made with Easy Toe.

39

Directions

Select the number of sts to CO based on the gauge for your yarn and needles and the circumference of the intended foot.

Stitch Table														
Foot Circumference in Inches														
5	5½	6	6½	7	7½	8	8½	9	9½	10	10½	11	11½	12
Gauge Sts/1" — Number of Stitches to CO														
5½		30			40				50			60	60		
6	30			40			50	50		60	60			70	70
6½			40			50			60			70	70		80
7		40			50			60			70		80	80	
7½				50			60			70		80			90
8	40		50			60		70	70		80		90	90	
8½				60					80		90			100	100
9		50		60		70		80			90		100		110
9½						70		80		90		100		110	
10	50		60		70	80			90		100		110		120

All 5-st patts have even number of sts so full-patt reps are on instep with equal number of sts on sole.

Short-Row Toe

For an alternative to short-row toe, see "Easy Toe" on page 42.

Using waste yarn and provisional CO (see page 22), CO 15 (20, 25, 30, 35, 40, 45, 50, 55, 60) sts. Purl 1 row with sock yarn.

Row 1 (RS): K13 (18, 23, 28, 33, 38, 43, 48, 53, 58), yf, sl next st, yb, PM, sl wrapped st back to LH needle, turn.

Row 2: P11 (16, 21, 26, 31, 36, 41, 46, 51, 56), yb, sl next st, yf, PM, sl wrapped st back to LH needle, turn.

Beg short-row shaping, slipping sts pwise unless otherwise instructed:

Row 3: Knit to st before last wrapped st, yf, sl next st, yb, PM, sl wrapped st back to LH needle, turn.

Row 4: Purl to st before last wrapped **st yb,** sl next **st, yf,** PM, sl wrapped st back to LH needle, turn.

Rep rows 3 and 4 until 7 (9, 11, 13, 15, 17, 19, 21, 23, 25) sts rem unwrapped, end by working WS row.

Reverse short-row shaping. Note that your short rows will be more attractive if you sl the wrap up and over the st before knitting it tog with the st.

Row 1 (RS): Knit to next wrapped st, (1 st before marker) knit this st tog with wrap, remove marker, yf, sl next st, yb, sl wrapped st back to LH needle, turn. This st now has 2 wraps.

Row 2: Purl to next wrapped st, (1 st before marker) purl this st tog with wrap, remove marker, yb, sl next st to RH needle, yf, return st to LH needle, turn.

Row 3: Knit to next wrapped st (1 st before marker), sl knit st to RH needle, PU wraps with LH needle and place on RH needle, sl all 3 sts back to LH needle, K3 tog, remove marker, yf, sl next st, yb, sl st back to LH needle, turn.

Row 4: Purl to next wrapped st (st before marker), sl purl st kwise, PU 2 wraps from base of st and place on RH needle over first slipped st, sl them back one at a time pwise to LH needle, P3tog in back of loop, remove marker, yb, sl next st pwise, yf, sl st back to LH needle, turn.

Rep rows 3 and 4 until you have worked all double wrapped sts and removed all markers.

The 2 end sts have 1 wrap each. Beg knitting in rnd, with RS facing you.

4 dpn	5 dpn	2 circular needles
Needle 1 (instep): K14 (19, 24, 29, 34, 39, 44, 49, 54, 59), knit next st tog with its wrap.	Needle 1 (instep): K5 (10, 10, 15, 15, 20, 20, 25, 25, 30). Needle 2 (instep): K9 (9, 14, 14, 19, 19, 24, 24, 29, 29), knit next st tog with its wrap.	Needle 1 (instep): K14 (19, 24, 29, 34, 39, 44, 49, 54, 59), knit next st tog with its wrap.
Unzip provisional CO and place sts on spare needle.		
Needle 2 (sole): K7 (10, 12, 15, 17, 20, 22, 25, 27, 30). Needle 3 (sole): K7 (9, 12, 14, 17, 19, 22, 24, 27, 28) from spare needle. Knit last st tog with its wrap. Sts per needle: (15, 7, 8), (20, 10, 10), (25, 12, 13), (30, 15, 15), (35, 17, 18), (40, 20, 20), (45, 22, 23), (50, 25, 25), (55, 27, 28), (60, 30, 30)	Needle 3 (sole): K7 (10, 12, 15, 17, 20, 22, 25, 27, 30). Needle 4 (sole): K7 (9, 12, 14, 17, 19, 22, 24, 27, 29) from spare needle. Knit last st tog with its wrap. Sts per needle: (5, 10, 7, 8), (10, 10, 10, 10), (10, 15, 12, 13), (15, 15, 15, 15), (15, 20, 17, 18), (20, 20, 20, 20), (20, 25, 22, 23), (25, 25, 25, 25), (25, 30, 27, 28), (30, 30, 30, 30)	Needle 2 (sole): K14 (19, 24, 29, 34, 39, 44, 49, 54, 59) from spare needle. Knit last st tog with its wrap. Sts per needle: 15 (20, 25, 30, 35, 40, 45, 50, 55, 60)

Instep and Sole

Needle 1: Beg patt st. Needles 2 and 3: Cont St st.	Needles 1 and 2: Beg patt st. Needles 3 and 4: Cont St st.	Needle 1: Beg patt st. Needle 2: Cont St st.

Cont on 30 (40, 50, 60, 70, 80, 90, 100, 110, 120) sts until sock reaches anklebone.

Short Row Heel

Note that working short-row heels with 3 needles helps reduce stretching of sts at spot where heel joins instep. The instructions include a lot of markers. When reversing short rows, markers help to keep things lined up. You can use ring markers or make your own. I used Knit Cro Sheen, but any smooth contrasting yarn will work fine. Cut short lengths and tie a knot to make a small ring.

Work heel back and forth in rows on 15 (20, 25, 30, 35, 40, 45, 50, 55, 60) sts.

Row 1 (RS): K13 (18, 23, 28, 33, 38, 43, 48, 53, 58), yf, sl next st, yb, PM, sl wrapped st back to LH needle, turn.

Row 2: P11 (16, 21, 26, 31, 36, 41, 46, 51, 56), yb, sl next st, yf, PM, sl wrapped st back to LH needle, turn.

Follow "Beg short-row shaping" on page 40, starting with row 3 and cont to the bottom of the page. Then cont with "Leg and Cuff" below.

Leg and Cuff

Needle 1 (instep): K14 (19, 24, 29, 34, 39, 44, 49, 54, 59), knit next st tog with its wrap.	Needle 1 (instep): K5 (10, 10, 15, 15, 20, 20, 25, 25, 30). Needle 2 (instep): K9 (9, 14, 14, 19, 19, 24, 24, 29, 29), knit next st tog with its wrap.	Needle 1 (instep): K14 (19, 24, 29, 34, 39, 44, 49, 54, 59), knit next st tog with its wrap.

Cont working est patt on instep. Work St st on bottom or back side of sock for 1", ending with last rnd of patt. Then beg working rnd 1 of est patt above the 1" of St st beyond heel, and work patt all around leg.

For those working with dpn, rearrange sts to make it easier to work in patt. Sts per needle:

(15, 5, 10), (20, 10, 10), (25, 10, 15), (30, 15, 15), (35, 15, 20), (40, 20, 20), (45, 20, 25), (50, 25, 25), (55, 25, 30), (60, 30, 30)	(5, 10, 5, 10), (10, 10, 10, 10), (10, 15, 10, 15), (15, 15, 15, 15), (15, 20, 15, 20), (20, 20, 20, 20), (20, 25, 20, 25), (25, 25, 25, 25), (25, 30, 25, 30), (30, 30, 30, 30)	N/A

Work est patt to desired leg length.

Cont knit and purl sequence in sock patt by working ribbing as follows: P1, *K3, P2, rep from * to last st, P1, or ribbing patt of choice. Work ribbing for 1½" or to desired cuff length.

Easy Toe

With waste yarn and provisional CO (see page 22), CO 6 (8, 10, 12, 14, 16, 18, 20, 22, 24) sts. Purl 1 row with sock yarn.

Work back and forth in St st for 6 rows or until rectangle is approx ½" high, end on a purl row. Unzip provisional CO sts and place them on spare needle. Beg knitting in rnd.

4 dpn	5 dpn	2 circular needles
With RS facing you, K6 (8, 10, 12, 14, 16, 18, 20, 22, 24), cont with needle 1, PU 2 sts from side edge. With needle 2, PU 2 sts from side edge, K3 (4, 5, 6, 7, 8, 9, 10, 11, 12). With needle 3, K3 (4, 5, 6, 7, 8, 9, 10, 11, 12) from spare needle, then PU 2 sts from side edge. With last needle, PU 2 sts from side edge, then knit rem sts from needle 1. Complete rnd by knitting across needles 2 and 3. Sts per needle: (10, 5, 5), (12, 6, 6), (14, 7, 7), (16, 8, 8), (18, 9, 9), (20, 10, 10), (22, 11, 11), (24, 12, 12), (26, 13, 13), (28, 14, 14)	With RS facing you, K3 (4, 5, 6, 7, 8, 9, 10, 11, 12); these sts will be part of needle 1. With needle 2, K3 (4, 5, 6, 7, 8, 9, 10, 11, 12) from needle, then PU 2 sts from side edge. With needle 3, PU 2 more sts from side edge, K3 (4, 5, 6, 7, 8, 9, 10, 11, 12) from CO. With needle 4, K3 (4, 5, 6, 7, 8, 9, 10, 11, 12) from CO edge and PU 2 sts from side edge. With needle 5, PU last 2 sts from side edge, knit first 3 sts; this is needle 1. Complete rnd by knitting across needles 2, 3, and 4. Sts per needle: 5 (6, 7, 8, 9, 10, 11, 12, 13, 14)	With RS facing you, K6 (8, 10, 12, 14, 16, 18, 20, 22, 24), cont with needle 1, PU 2 sts from side edge. With needle 2, PU 2 sts from side edge, K6 (8, 10, 12, 14, 16, 18, 20, 22, 24) from CO edge, PU 2 sts from side edge. With needle 1, PU 2 sts from side edge. Complete rnd by knitting across rem sts on needle 1 and across needle 2. Sts per needle: 10 (12, 14, 16, 18, 20, 22, 24, 26, 28)

Beg toe inc as follows:

Rnd 1	Rnd 1	Rnd 1
Needle 1: K1, M1, knit to last st, M1, K1. Needle 2: K1, M1, knit to end. Needle 3: Knit to last st, M1, K1.	Needle 1: K1, M1, knit to end. Needle 2: Knit to last st, M1, K1. Needle 3: K1, M1, knit to end. Needle 4: Knit to last st, M1, K1.	Needle 1: K1, M1, knit to last st, M1, K1. Needle 2: K1, M1, knit to last st, M1, K1.

Rnd 2: Knit.

Rep rnds 1 and 2 until 28 (40, 48, 60, 68, 80, 88, 100, 108, 120) total sts rem.

Note that if you're working a sock with 30, 50, 70, 90, or 110 sts for foot circumference, work rnd 3 as follows:

Rnd 3	Rnd 3	Rnd 3
Needle 1: Knit to last st, M1, K1. Needle 2: Knit 1, M1, knit to end. Needle 3: Knit.	Needle 1: Knit. Needle 2: Knit 1, M1, knit to end. Needle 3: Knit to last st, M1, K1. Needle 4: Knit.	Needle 1: Knit to last st, M1, K1. Needle 2: K1, M1, knit to end.

Cont with "Instep and Sole" on page 41.

Stitch Dictionary

Instructions are for working patterns in the round. All rows of charts are worked from right to left and from bottom to top. Note that most of the patterns begin and end with P1 so that the patterns will be centered on the instep; Seed St Rib begins and ends with K1.

Yarn over Cable

Rnd 1: *P1, sl 1, K2, psso, P1, rep from *.
Rnd 2: *P1, K1, YO, K1, P1, rep from *.
Rnds 3 and 4: *P1, K3, P1, rep from *.
Rep rnds 1–4.

Laburnum

Rnds 1, 2: *P1, K3, P1, rep from *.
Rnd 3: *P1, K3tog, YO, P1, rep from *.
Rnd 4: *P1, K1, knit in front and then back of YO, P1, rep from *.
Rep rnds 1–4.

Beaded Rib

Rnd 1: *P1, K1, P1, K1, P1, rep from *.
Rnd 2: *P1, K3, P1, rep from *.
Rep rnds 1 and 2.

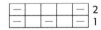

Little Shell Rib

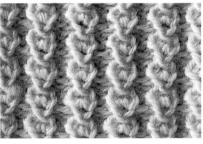

Rnds 1, 2: *P1, K3, P1, rep from *.
Rnd 3: *P1, sl 1, K2tog, psso, P1, rep from *.
Rnd 4: *P1, (K1, P1, K1) in front of next st, P1, rep from *.
Rep rnds 1–4.

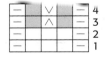

Willow Buds

Rnds 1, 3: *P1, K3, P1, rep from *.
Rnd 2: *P1, P3 tog, knit same 3 sts tog, purl same 3 sts tog again, and sl all 3 sts from needle, P1, rep from *.
Rnd 4: *P1, K3, P1, rep from *.
Rep rnds 1–4.

Lace Rib

Rnd 1, 3: *P1, K3, P1, rep from *.
Rnd 2: *P1, K1, YO, ssk, P1, rep from *.
Rnd 4: *P1, K2tog, YO, K1, P1, rep from *.
Rep rnds 1–4.

Six-Stitch Patterns

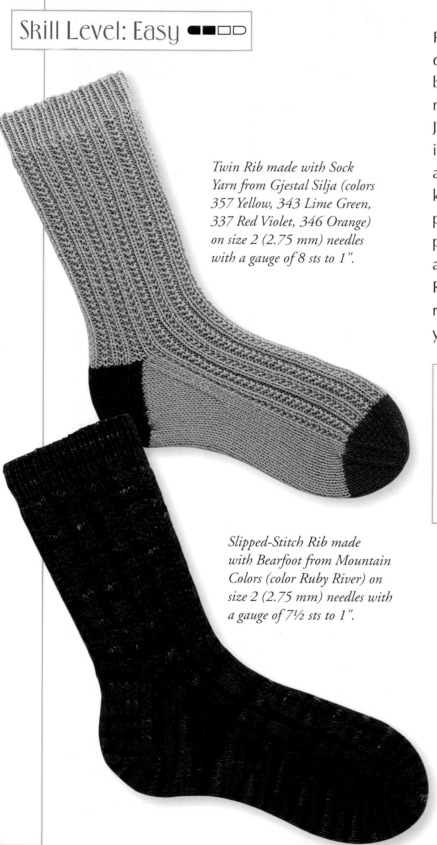

Skill Level: Easy ■■□□

Twin Rib made with Sock Yarn from Gjestal Silja (colors 357 Yellow, 343 Lime Green, 337 Red Violet, 346 Orange) on size 2 (2.75 mm) needles with a gauge of 8 sts to 1".

Slipped-Stitch Rib made with Bearfoot from Mountain Colors (color Ruby River) on size 2 (2.75 mm) needles with a gauge of 7½ sts to 1".

Patterns in this section are the classic top-down, heel-flap socks. As knitting patterns become wider, it's possible to make socks more visually complex and interesting. Just because the patterns look complex, it doesn't mean they are—some of them are only 2 rounds high and a pleasure to knit. There are a variety of structures for patterns that are 6 stitches wide. I find that patterns based on a *knit 3, purl 3* ribbing are most intriguing. The Slipped-Stitch Rib pattern is one that helps break up the repeat sequence in some hand-painted yarns, a bonus for some of us.

Materials

Referring to "Sock Yarn" and "Sock Basics" on pages 8–17, gather materials for the socks you'd like to make.

Ring markers (for 2 circular needles technique)

Directions

Select the number of sts to CO based on the gauge for your yarn and needles and the circumference of the intended foot.

Stitch Table															
Gauge Sts/1"	**Foot Circumference in Inches**														
	5	5½	6	6½	7	7½	8	8½	9	9½	10	10½	11	11½	12
	Number of Stitches to CO														
5½		30				42			54	54				66	66
6	30				42				54				66		
6½			42					54			66	66		78	78
7			42			54	54			66			78		
7½		42			54				66			78			90
8								66		78	78		90	90	
8½	42			54			66		78			90			102
9			54			66		78			90	102	102		
9½		54			66		78			90		102			114
10	54			66					90		102			114	

The sock stitches are all a multiple of 12 + 6. The extra sts are required to balance the patt on instep.

Cuff and Leg

Using long-tail CO method, CO 30 (42, 54, 66, 78, 90, 102, 114) sts. Divide sts per needle as follows:

4 dpn	5 dpn	2 circular needles
(6, 9, 15), (9, 12, 21), (12, 15, 27), (15, 18, 33), (18, 21, 39), (21, 24, 45), (24, 27, 51), (27, 30, 57)	(6, 9, 6, 9), (9, 12, 9, 12), (12, 15, 12, 15), (15, 18, 15, 18), (18, 21, 18, 21), (21, 24, 21, 24), (24, 27, 24, 27), (27, 30, 27, 30)	15 (21, 27, 33, 39, 45, 51, 57)

Join, being careful not to twist sts, and work K1, P1 ribbing for 1½".
Beg patt of choice and work to desired leg length.

Heel Flap

Heel is worked back and forth in rows on 15 (21, 27, 33, 39, 45, 51, 57) sts beg with WS row and ending with RS row.

Needles 1 and 2: Instep sts Needle 3: Heel sts	Needles 1 and 2: Instep sts Combine sts on needles 3 and 4 to needle 3.	Needle 1: Instep sts Needle 2: Heel sts

Remember, you *must* turn your work to beg heel flap!
   Row 1 (WS): K1, purl to last st, sl 1 wyif.
   Row 2: *K1, sl 1 wyib, rep from * to last st, sl 1 wyif. There will be 2 slipped sts next to each other, the first slipped with yarn in back and the last st with yarn in front.
   Rep rows 1 and 2 until you have 16 (22, 28, 34, 40, 46, 52, 58) heel-flap rows; the last row should be a RS row, and heel-flap shape should be close to square.

Heel Turn

Row 1 (WS): Sl 1, P8 (11, 14, 17, 20, 23, 26, 29) sts, P2tog, P1, turn.
Row 2: Sl 1, K4, ssk, K1, turn.
Row 3: Sl 1, purl to within 1 st of gap, P2tog (1 st on either side of gap), P1, turn.
Row 4: Sl 1, knit to within 1 st of gap, ssk, K1, turn.
Rep rows 3 and 4, inc 1 additional knit or purl st after the sl 1 until all side sts are worked, end with RS (knit) row—9 (13, 15, 19, 21, 25, 27, 31) sts left on heel flap.
Because you have an odd number of sts, divide heel-flap sts as follows:

4 dpn	5 dpn	2 circular needles
Sl 4 (6, 7, 9, 10, 12, 13, 14) sts from RH side of heel sts to needle 4. LH needle is needle 1.	Sl 4 (6, 7, 9, 10, 12, 13, 14) sts from RH side of heel sts to needle 5. LH needle is needle 1.	Renumber needles: Needle 1: Heel sts Needle 2: Instep sts

Gusset

With needle 1, PU 8 (11, 14, 17, 20, 23, 26, 29) sts from side of heel flap. PU 2 extra sts at top of gusset (see page 25), then:

Work in patt across needle 2 (instep), beg where you left off in patt to work heel. Needle 3: PU 2 extra sts at top of gusset, PU 8 (11, 14, 17, 20, 23, 26, 29) sts from side of heel flap, knit rem heel-flap sts onto needle 3.	Work in patt across needles 2 and 3 (instep), beg where you left off in patt to work heel. Needle 4: PU 2 extra sts at top of gusset, PU 8 (11, 14, 17, 20, 23, 26, 29) sts from side of heel flap, knit rem heel-flap sts onto needle 4.	Cont with needle 1: PM, work 6 (9, 12, 15, 18, 21, 24, 27) sts in patt. Needle 2: Work rem instep sts, PM, PU 2 extra sts at top of gusset, PU 8 (11, 14, 17, 20, 23, 26, 29) sts from side of heel flap, knit rem 5 (7, 8, 10, 11, 13, 14, 15) heel-flap sts onto needle 1.

Gusset Decrease

Work rnd 1 once to combine picked-up sts and to eliminate gap at top of gusset.

Rnd 1	Rnd 1	Rnd 1
Needle 1: Knit to last 2 sts, ssk. Needle 2: Work est patt. Needle 3: K2tog, knit to end.	Needle 1: Knit to last 2 sts, ssk. Needles 2 and 3: Work est patt. Needle 4: K2tog, knit to end.	Needle 1: Knit to 2 sts before marker, ssk, SM, work est patt to end. Needle 2: Work est patt to marker, SM, K2tog, knit to end.
Rnd 2 (dec rnd) Needle 1: Knit to last 3 sts, K2tog, K1. Needle 2: Work est patt. Needle 3: K1, ssk, knit to end.	**Rnd 2 (dec rnd)** Needle 1: Knit to last 3 sts, K2tog, K1. Needles 2 and 3: Work est patt. Needle 4: K1, ssk, knit to end.	**Rnd 2 (dec rnd)** Needle 1: Knit to 3 sts before marker, K2tog, K1, SM, work est patt to end. Needle 2: Work est patt to marker, SM, K1, ssk, knit to end.
Rnd 3 Needle 1: Knit. Needle 2: Work est patt. Needle 3: Knit.	**Rnd 3** Needle 1: Knit. Needles 2 and 3: Work est patt. Needle 4: Knit.	**Rnd 3** Needle 1: Knit to marker, SM, work est patt. Needle 2: Work est patt to marker, SM, knit to end.

Rep rnds 2 and 3 until 30 (42, 54, 66, 78, 90, 102, 114) total sts rem.

Foot		
4 dpn	**5 dpn**	**2 circular needles**
Cont St st on needles 1 and 3 and est patt on needle 2 to desired heel-to-toe length.	Cont St st on needles 1 and 4 and est patt on needles 2 and 3 to desired heel-to-toe length.	Rearrange sts so instep sts are on needle 1 and sole sts are on needle 2. Cont St st on needle 2 and est patt on needle 1 to desired heel-to-toe length.
Toe Shaping		
Work sts on needle 1. Beg of rnd has shifted; renumber needles. For toe instructions, instep sts will now be on needle 1, and sole sts on needles 2 and 3. **Rnd 1** Needle 1: K1, ssk, knit to last 3 sts, K2tog, K1. Needle 2: K1, ssk, knit to end. Needle 3: Knit to last 3 sts, K2tog, K1.	Work sts on needle 1. Beg of rnd has shifted; renumber needles. For toe instructions, instep sts will now be on needles 1 and 2, and sole sts on needles 3 and 4. **Rnd 1** Needle 1: K1, ssk, knit to end. Needle 2: Knit to last 3 sts, K2tog, K1. Needle 3: K1, ssk, knit to end. Needle 4: Knit to last 3 sts, K2tog, K1.	**Rnd 1** Needle 1: K1, ssk, knit to last 3 sts, K2tog, K1. Needle 2: K1, ssk, knit to last 3 sts, K2tog, K1.

Rnd 2: Knit around.

Rep rnds 1 and 2 until 14 (22, 26, 34, 38, 46, 50, 58) total sts rem.
Rep rnd 1 only until 10 (14, 14, 18, 22, 22, 26, 30) total sts rem.
Place sts from top of sock on 1 needle and sts from bottom onto 2nd needle. Graft toe sts tog with kitchener st (see page 24).

Stitch Dictionary

Instructions are for working patterns in the round. All rows of charts are worked from right to left and from bottom to top.

Twin Rib

Rnd 1: *K3, P3, rep from *.
Rnd 2: *K1, P1, rep from *.
Rep rnds 1 and 2.

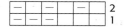

Slipped-Stitch Rib

Rnd 1: *K3, P3, rep from *.
Rnd 2: *K1, sl 1 wyib, K1, P1, sl 1 wyif, P1, rep from *.
Rep rnds 1 and 2.

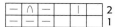

Stansfield #10

Rnd 1: *K3, P3, rep from *.
Rnd 2: *K3, P1, K1, P1, rep from *.
Rnd 3: *P4, K1, P1, rep from *.
Rnd 4: *K3, P1, K1, P1, rep from *.
Rep rnds 1–4.

Stansfield #11

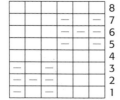

Rnds 1, 3: *K3, P1, K1, P1, rep from *.
Rnd 2: *K3, P3, rep from *.
Rnd 4: Knit.
Rnds 5, 7: *P1, K1, P1, K3, rep from *.
Rnd 6: *P3, K3, rep from *.
Rnd 8: Knit.
Rep rnds 1–8.

Cloverleaf Eyelet Cable

Rnds 1, 3, 5: *K3, P3, rep from *.
Rnd 2: *YO, sl 1, K2tog, psso, YO, P3, rep from *.
Rnd 4: *K1, YO, ssk, P3, rep from *.
Rnd 6: *K3, P3, rep from *.
Rep rnds 1–6.

Chain Rib

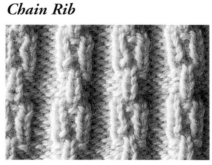

Rnds 1, 5, 6: *K3, P3, rep from *.
Rnds 2, 3, 4: *K1, P1, K1, P3, rep from *.
Rnds 7, 8, 9: *P1, K1, P4, rep from *.
Rnd 10: *K3, P3, rep from *.
Rep rnds 1–10.

Open Rib

Rnds 1, 2, 3: *K3, P1, K1, P1, rep from *.
Rnd 4: *YO, sl 1, K2tog, psso, YO, P1, K1, P1, rep from *.
Rep rnds 1–4.

Waterfall Rib

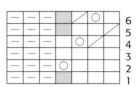

Rnd 1: *K3, P3, rep from *.
Rnd 2: *K3, YO, P3, rep from *.
Rnd 3: *K4, P3, rep from *.
Rnd 4: *K1, K2tog, YO, K1, P3, rep from *.
Rnd 5: *K2tog, K2, P3, rep from *.
Rnd 6: *K1, YO, K2tog, P3, rep from *.
Rep rnds 1–6.

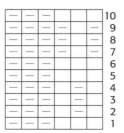

Moorish Lattice

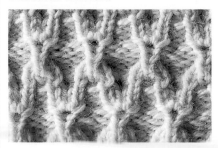

Rnds 1, 2, 3: *K3, P3, rep from *.
Rnd 4: *Sl 2, K1, p2sso, P3, rep from *.
Rnd 5: *K1, P3, rep from *.
Rnd 6: *(K1, YO, K1) in next st, P3, rep from *.
Rnds 7, 8, 9: *K3, P3, rep from *.
Rnd 10: *K1, (K1, YO, K1) in next st, K1, P3tog, rep from *.
Rnds 11, 12, 13: *P3, K3, rep from *.
Rnd 14: *P3, sl 2, K1, P2sso, rep from *.
Rnd 15: *P3, K1, rep from *.
Rnd 16: *P3, (K1, YO, K1) in next st, rep from *.
Rnds 17, 18, 19: *P3, K3, rep from *.
Rnd 20: *P3tog, K1, (K1, YO, K1) in next st, K1, rep from *.
Rep rnds 1–20.

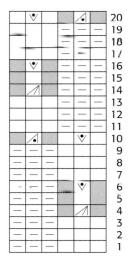

Harebell Lace

Rnds 1, 3, 5: *K3, P3, rep from *.
Rnd 2: *K3, P2tog, YO, P1, rep from *.
Rnd 4: *K3, P1, YO, P2tog, rep from *.
Rnd 6: *Sl 2, K1, P2sso, (P1, YO) twice, P1, rep from *.
Rnds 7, 9, 11: *P3, K3, rep from *.
Rnd 8: *P1, YO, P2tog, K3, rep from *.
Rnd 10: *P2tog, YO, P1, K3, rep from *.
Rnd 12: *(P1, YO) twice, P1, sl 2, K1, P2sso, rep from *.
Rep rnds 1–12.

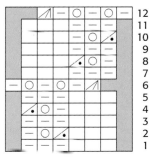

Bluebell Rib

Rnds 1, 2, 3, 4: *K3, P3, rep from *.
Rnd 5: *YO, sl 1, K2tog, psso, YO, P3, rep from *.
Rnd 6: *K3, P3, rep from *.
Rep rnds 1–6.

Eight-Stitch Patterns

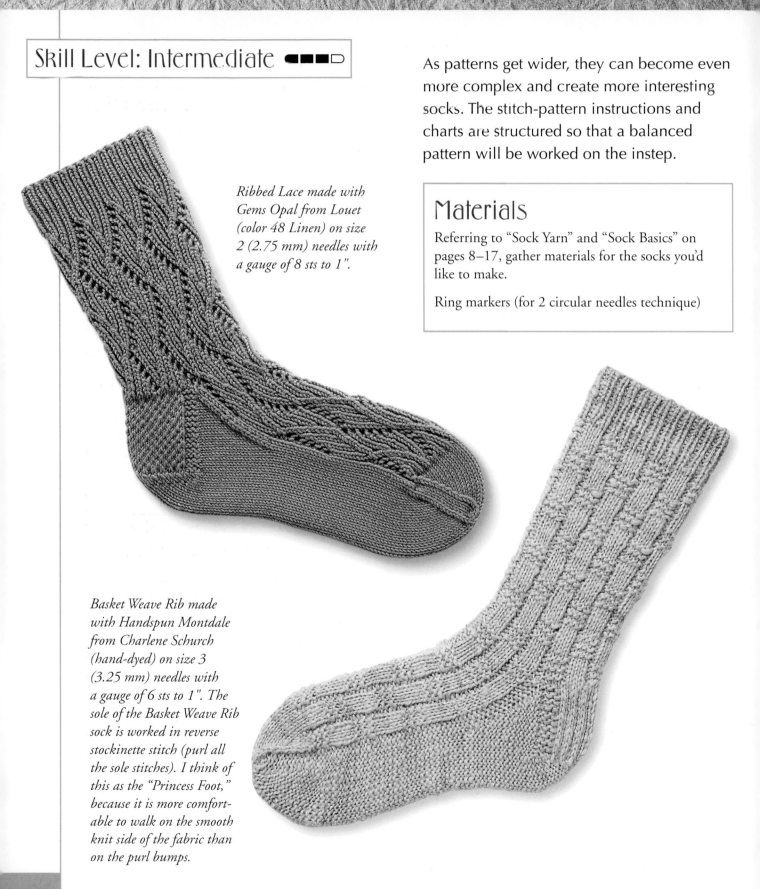

Skill Level: Intermediate ◀■■■▷

As patterns get wider, they can become even more complex and create more interesting socks. The stitch-pattern instructions and charts are structured so that a balanced pattern will be worked on the instep.

Ribbed Lace made with Gems Opal from Louet (color 48 Linen) on size 2 (2.75 mm) needles with a gauge of 8 sts to 1".

Materials

Referring to "Sock Yarn" and "Sock Basics" on pages 8–17, gather materials for the socks you'd like to make.

Ring markers (for 2 circular needles technique)

Basket Weave Rib made with Handspun Montdale from Charlene Schurch (hand-dyed) on size 3 (3.25 mm) needles with a gauge of 6 sts to 1". The sole of the Basket Weave Rib sock is worked in reverse stockinette stitch (purl all the sole stitches). I think of this as the "Princess Foot," because it is more comfortable to walk on the smooth knit side of the fabric than on the purl bumps.

Directions

Select the number of sts to CO based on the gauge for your yarn and needles and the circumference of the intended foot.

Stitch Table															
	Foot Circumference in Inches														
Gauge Sts/1"	5	5½	6	6½	7	7½	8	8½	9	9½	10	10½	11	11½	12
	Number of Stitches to CO														
5½			32				48	40						64	
6		32			48							64	64		
6½	32			48					64	64					80
7			48				64						80	80	
7½				48				64				80			
8			48			64					80				96
8½		48			64					80			96	96	
9				64				80			96				
9½	48						80			96				112	112
10				64			80			96			112		

Cuff and Leg

Using long-tail CO method, CO 32 (48, 64, 80, 96, 112) sts. Divide sts per needle as follows:

4 dpn	5 dpn	2 circular needles
(8, 8, 16), (12, 12, 24), (16, 16, 32), (20, 20, 40), (24, 24, 48), (28, 28, 56)	8 (12, 16, 20, 24, 28)	16 (24, 32, 40, 48, 56)

Join, being careful not to twist sts, and work K1, P1 ribbing for 1½". Work in patt of choice to desired leg length. Just work 8-st pattern—the extra st at beg of chart will be used when working instep of foot.

Heel Flap

Heel is worked back and forth in rows on 15 (23, 31, 39, 47, 55) sts, beg with WS row and ending with RS row. Unknit last st of rnd and move to beg of rnd to balance patt on instep.

Heel worked on needle 3.	Sl sts from needle 4 to needle 3 to work on heel flap. Set needle 4 aside. Heel worked on needle 3.	Heel worked on needle 2.
Sts per needle:		
(9, 8, 15), (13, 12, 23), (17, 16, 31), (21, 20, 39), (25, 24, 47), (29, 28, 55)	(9, 8, 15), (13, 12, 23), (17, 16, 31), (21, 20, 39), (25, 24, 47), (29, 28, 55)	(17, 15), (25, 23), (33, 31), (41, 39), (49, 47), (57, 55)

Turn work to beg working heel with WS row.

Heel for Ribbed Lace sock:

Eye of Partridge heel patt, with garter edging

Rows 1 and 3 (WS): K3, purl to end of row.

Row 2: P3, *K1, sl 1, rep from * to last 4 sts, K4.

Row 4: P3, *sl 1, K1, rep across to last 4 sts, sl 1, K3.

Rep rows 1–4 until you have 16 (24, 32, 40, 48, 56) heel-flap rows, end by working RS row.

Heel for Basket Weave Rib sock:

Heel-st patt

Row 1 (WS): K3, purl to end.

Row 2: P3, *K1, sl 1, rep from * to last 4 sts, K4.

Rep rows 1 and 2 until you have 16 (24, 32, 40, 48, 56) heel-flap rows, end by working RS row.

Heel Turn

Work as follows:

Row 1 (WS): Sl 1, P8 (12, 16, 20, 24, 28) sts, P2tog, P1, turn.

Row 2: Sl 1, K4, ssk, K1, turn.

Row 3: Sl 1, purl to within 1 st of gap, P2tog (1 st on either side of gap), P1, turn.

Row 4: Sl 1, knit to within 1 st of gap, ssk, K1, turn.

Rep rows 3 and 4, inc 1 additional knit or purl st after sl 1 until all side sts are worked, end with RS (knit) row—9 (13, 17, 21, 25, 29) sts left on heel flap.

For ease of instructions, beg of rnd is now at center of bottom of foot. The needles are renumbered at this point. Needle 1 is beg of rnd.

4 dpn	5 dpn	2 circular needles
Sl 4 (6, 8, 10, 12, 14) sts from RH side of heel sts to needle 4. LH needle is needle 1.	Sl 4 (6, 8, 10, 12, 14) sts from RH side of heel sts to needle 5. LH needle is needle 1.	Needle 1: Heel sts Needle 2: Instep sts

Gusset

Cont with needle 1, PU 8 (12, 16, 20, 24, 28) sts from side of heel flap, PU 2 sts at top of gusset (see page 25). At this point, beg working **extra st** at beg of instep from chart or written instructions.

Needle 2: Work across instep in est patt. Needle 3: PU 2 sts at top of gusset, PU 8 (12, 16, 20, 24, 28) sts from side of heel flap, knit rem heel sts. Sts per needle: (15, 17, 14), (21, 25, 20), (27, 33, 26), (33, 41, 32), (39, 49, 38), (45, 57, 44)	Needles 2 and 3: Work across instep in est patt. Needle 4: PU 2 sts at top of gusset, PU 8 (12, 16, 20, 24, 28) sts from side of heel flap, knit rem heel sts. Sts per needle: (15, 8, 9, 14), (21, 8, 17, 20), (27, 16, 17, 26), (33, 16, 25, 32), (39, 24, 25, 38), (45, 24, 33, 44)	Cont with needle 1, PM, K9 (13, 17, 21, 25, 29) instep sts from needle 2. Needle 2: Work remainder of instep sts, PM, PU 2 sts at top of gusset, PU 8 (12, 16, 20, 24, 28) sts from side of heel flap 4, (6, 8, 10, 12, 14) heel sts from needle 1 to needle 2. Sts per needle: (23, 23), (29, 37), (43, 43), (49, 57), (63, 63), (69, 77) We've shifted from needles holding front and back of sock to left and right sides.

There are an odd number of sts on instep. The extra st will balance patt of instep. It's easier to work with complete patts plus extra st rather than having sts divided evenly with part of patt on one instep needle and balance on another.

Gusset Decrease

4 dpn	5 dpn	2 circular needles
Work rnd 1 once to combine sts picked up and to eliminate gap at top of gusset.		
Rnd 1 Needle 1: Knit to last 2 sts, ssk. Needle 2: Work est patt. Needle 3: K2tog, knit to end.	**Rnd 1** Needle 1: Knit to last 2 sts, ssk. Needles 2 and 3: Work est patt. Needle 4: K2tog, knit to end.	**Rnd 1** Needle 1: Knit to 2 sts before marker, ssk, SM, work est patt to end. Needle 2: Work est patt to marker, SM, K2tog, knit to end.
Rnd 2 (dec rnd) Needle 1: Knit to last 3 sts, K2tog, K1. Needle 2: Work est patt. Needle 3: K1, ssk, knit around.	**Rnd 2 (dec rnd)** Needle 1: Knit to last 3 sts, K2tog, K1. Needles 2 and 3: Work est patt. Needle 4: K1, ssk, knit around.	**Rnd 2 (dec rnd)** Needle 1: Knit to 3 sts before marker, K2tog, K1, SM, work est patt to end. Needle 2: Work est patt to marker, SM, K1, ssk, knit to end.
Rnd 3 Needle 1: Knit. Needle 2: Work est patt. Needle 3: Knit.	**Rnd 3** Needle 1: Knit. Needles 2 and 3: Work est patt. Needle 4: Knit.	**Rnd 3** Needle 1: Knit to marker, SM, work est patt. Needle 2: Work est patt to marker, SM, knit to end.
Rep rnds 2 and 3 until 32 (48, 64, 80, 96, 112) total sts rem.		

Foot

4 dpn	5 dpn	2 circular needles
Cont St st on needles 1 and 3, and est patt on needle 2, to desired heel-to-toe length.	Cont St st on needles 1 and 4, and est patt on needles 2 and 3, to desired heel-to-toe length.	Rearrange sts so that all instep sts are on needle 1, and all sole sts are on needle 2. Cont est patt on needle 1, and St st on needle 2 to desired heel-to-toe length.

Toe Shaping

4 dpn	5 dpn	2 circular needles
Knit sts on needle 1. Beg of round has shifted; renumber needles. For toe instructions, instep sts will now be on needle 1, and sole sts on needles 2 and 3.	Knit sts on needle 1. Beg of round has shifted; renumber needles. For toe instructions, instep sts will now be on needles 1 and 2, and sole sts on needles 3 and 4.	Needle 1: Instep sts Needle 2: Sole sts
Sts should be divided per needle as follows:		
(17, 8, 7), (25, 12, 11), (33, 16, 15), (41, 20, 19), (49, 24, 23), (57, 28, 27)	(9, 8, 8, 7), (13, 12, 12, 11), (17, 16, 16, 15), (21, 20, 20, 19), (25, 24, 24, 23), (29, 28, 28, 27)	(17, 15), (25, 23), (33, 31), (41, 39), (49, 47), (57, 55)
Rnd 1 Needle 1: K1, ssk, knit to last 3 sts, K2tog, K1. Needle 2: K1, ssk, knit to end. Needle 3: Knit to last 3 sts, K2tog, K1.	**Rnd 1** Needle 1: K1, ssk, knit to end. Needle 2: Knit to last 3 sts, K2tog, K1. Needle 3: K1, ssk, knit to end. Needle 4: Knit to last 3 sts, K2tog, K1.	**Rnd 1** Needle 1: K1, ssk, knit to last 3 sts, K2tog, K1. Needle 2: K1, ssk, knit to last 3 sts, K2tog, K1.

Rnd 2: Knit.

Rep rnds 1 and 2 until 16 (24, 32, 40, 48, 56) total sts rem.

Rep rnd 1 only until 10 (14, 18, 22, 26, 30) total sts rem. You'll end by working last dec rnd on instep. You'll have even number of total sts but an odd number of sts on instep and sole.

Place sts from top of sock on 1 needle and sts from bottom onto 2nd needle. Graft toe sts tog with kitchener st (see page 24).

Stitch Dictionary

Instructions are for working patterns in the round. All rows of charts are worked from right to left and from bottom to top. The written instructions begin with a stitch (indicated in brackets) and the charts begin with a separate column. This extra stitch is worked only once at the beginning of the instep. When working the leg, work only the 8-stitch repeats. The extra stitch has been added to balance the total pattern on the instep.

Ribbed Lace

Rnd 1: [P1], *YO, ssk, (K1, P1) 3 times, rep from *.

Rnd 2: [P1], *K3, (P1, K1) twice, P1, rep from *.

Rnd 3: [P1], *YO, P1, ssk, (P1, K1) twice, P1, rep from *.

Rnds 4, 8, 12, 16, 20: [P1], *(K1, P1) 4 times, rep from *.

Rnd 5: [P1], *YO, K1, P1, ssk, (K1, P1) twice, rep from *.

Rnd 6: [P1], *(K2, P1) 2 times, K1, P1, rep from *.

Rnd 7: [P1], *YO, P1, K1, P1, ssk, P1, K1, P1, rep from *.

Rnd 9: [P1], *YO, (K1, P1) twice, ssk, K1, P1, rep from *.

Rnd 10: [P1], *K2, P1, K1, P1, K2, P1, rep from *.

Rnd 11: [P1], *YO, (P1, K1) twice, P1, ssk, P1, rep from *.

Rnd 13: [P1], *(K1, P1) twice, K1, K2tog, YO, P1, rep from *.

Rnd 14: [P1], *(K1, P1) twice, K3, P1, rep from *.

Rnd 15: [P1], *(K1, P1) twice, K2tog, P1, YO, P1, rep from *.

Rnd 17: [P1], *K1, P1, K1, K2tog, P1, K1, YO, P1, rep from *.

Rnd 18: [P1], *K1, (P1, K2) twice, P1, rep from *.

Rnd 19: [P1], *K1, P1, K2tog, P1, K1, P1, YO, P1, rep from *.

Rnd 21: [P1], *K1, K2tog, (P1, K1) twice, YO, P1, rep from *.

Rnd 22: [P1], *K1, (K1, P1) twice, K2, P1, rep from *.

Rnd 23: [P1], *K2tog, (P1, K1) twice, P1, YO, P1, rep from *.

Rnd 24: [P1], *(K1, P1) 4 times, rep from *.

Rep rnds 1–24.

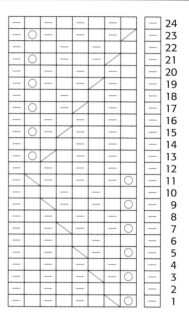

Basket Weave Rib

Rnds 1, 3, 5, 7, 9, 11: [P1], *(K3, P1) twice, rep from *.

Rnds 2, 4, 6: [P1], *P4, K3, P1, rep from *.

Rnds 8, 10, 12: [P1], *K3, P5, rep from *.

Rep rnds 1–12.

Diamond Rib

Rnd 1: [P1], *K2tog, (K1, YO) twice, K1, ssk, P1, rep from *.

Rnds 2, 4, 6: [P1], *K7, P1, rep from *.

Rnd 3: [P1], *K2tog, YO, K3, YO, ssk, P1, rep from *.

Rnd 5: [P1], *K1, YO, ssk, K1, K2tog, YO, K1, P1, rep from *.

Rnd 7: [P1], *K2, YO, sl 1, K2tog, psso, YO, K2, P1, rep from *.

Rnd 8: [P1], *K7, P1, rep from *.

Rep rnds 1–8.

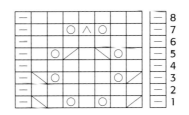

Oblique Openwork

Rnd 1: [P1], *P1, YO, ssk, K1, YO, ssk, P2, rep from *.

Rnds 2, 4: [P1], *P1, K5, P2, rep from *.

Rnd 3: [P1], *P1, K1, YO, ssk, K2, P2, rep from *.

Rnd 5: [P1], *P1, K2, YO, ssk, K1, P2, rep from *.

Rnd 6: [P1], *P1, K5, P2, rep from *.

Rep rnds 1–6.

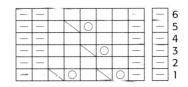

Traveling Rib Eyelet

Rnds 1, 3, 5, 7, 8, 9, 11, 13, 15: [P1], *P1, K5, P2, rep from *.

Rnds 2, 4, 6: [P1], *P1, YO, ssk, K1, K2tog, YO, P2, rep from *.

Rnds 10, 12, 14: [P1], *P1, K2tog, YO, K1, YO, ssk, P2, rep from *.

Rnd 16: [P1], *P1, K5, P2, rep from *.

Rep rnds 1–16.

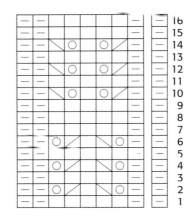

Arrow

Rnds 1, 3, 5: [K1], knit.

Rnd 2: [K1], *YO, ssk, K3, K2tog, YO, K1, rep from *.

Rnd 4: [K1], *K1, YO, ssk, K1, K2tog, YO, K2, rep from *.

Rnd 6: [P1], *K2, YO, sl 1, K2tog, psso, YO, K2, P1, rep from *.

Rnds 7, 9, 11, 13, 15: [P1], *K7, P1, rep from *.

Rnds 8, 10, 12, 14, 16: [P1], *SSK, K1, YO, K1-b, YO, K1, K2tog, P1, rep from *.

Rep rnds 1–16.

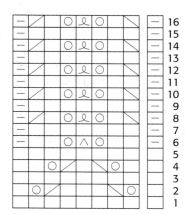

Textured Rib

Rnds 1, 2, 3, 4: [K1], *P2, K3, P2, K1, rep from *.

Rnds 5, 6, 7, 8: [K1], *K1, P2, K1, P2, K2, rep from *.

Rep rnds 1–8.

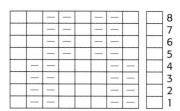

Twelve-Stitch Patterns

The Small Capitals and Oriel are strong directional patterns that look better when worked from the bottom to the top of a knitted piece, so these socks are knit from the toe up. The heel flap is on the bottom of the foot, providing a longer area to work more densely on a smaller needle or with reinforcing thread.

Materials

Referring to "Sock Yarn" and "Sock Basics" on pages 8–17, gather materials for the socks you'd like to make.

Ring markers (for 2 circular needles technique)

Oriel made with Froehlich Special Blauband from Froehlich Wolle (color 88 Teal) on size 1 (2.25 mm) needles with a gauge of 8 sts to 1". This sock is made with Easy Toe.

Small Capitals made with Gems Opal from Louet (color 26 Crab Apple Blossom) on size 2 (2.75 mm) needles with a gauge of 7 sts to 1". This sock is made with Round Toe.

Directions

Select the number of sts to CO based on the gauge for your yarn and needles and the circumference of the intended foot.

Stitch Table															
Gauge Sts/1"	**Foot Circumference in Inches**														
	5	5½	6	6½	7	7½	8	8½	9	9½	10	10½	11	11½	12
	Number of Stitches to CO														
5									48	48					
5½								48							
6							48								72
6½						48							72	72	
7					48						72	72			
7½				48						72					
8			48						72						96
8½		48						72					96	96	
9							72					96			
9½	48					72					96				
10										96					120

Easy Toe		
For alternate "Round-Toe Cast On," see page 61.		
With waste yarn and provisional CO (see page 22), CO 10 (14, 20, 24) sts. Purl 1 row with sock yarn. Work back and forth in St st for 6 rows or until rectangle is approx ½" high, ending on a purl row. Unzip provisional CO sts and place them on needles as follows:		
4 dpn	**5 dpn**	**2 circular needles**
Needle 4. Beg knitting in rnd.	Needle 5. Beg knitting in rnd.	Needle 2.
Needle 1: With RS facing you, K10 (14, 20, 24), cont with needle 1, PU 2 sts from side edge.	Needle 1: With RS facing you, K5 (7, 10, 12); these sts will be part of needle 1.	Needle 1: With RS facing you, K10 (14, 20, 24), PU 2 sts from side edge; these sts are part of needle 1.
Needle 2: PU 2 sts from side edge, K5 (7, 10, 12) from needle 4.	Needle 2: K5 (7, 10, 12) from needle 5, then PU 2 sts from side edge.	Needle 2: PU 2 sts from side edge, K10 (14, 20, 24) sts from CO edge, PU 2 sts from side edge.
Needle 3: K5 (7, 10, 12) from needle 4, PU 2 sts from side edge.	Needle 3: PU 2 sts from side edge, K5 (7, 10, 12) from needle 5.	Needle 1: PU 2 sts from side edge.
Needle 4: PU 2 sts from side edge, knit sts from needle 1.	Needle 4: K5 (7, 10, 12) from needle 5, PU 2 sts from side edge.	Sts per needle: 14 (18, 24, 28).
Sts per needle: (14, 7, 7), (18, 9, 9), (24, 12, 12), (28, 14, 14).	Needle 5: PU 2 sts from side edge, knit first 5 sts; this is needle 1.	Complete rnd by knitting across rem needle 1 sts and across needle 2.
Complete rnd by knitting across needles 2 and 3.	Sts per needle: 7 (9, 12, 14).	
	Complete rnd by knitting across needles 2, 3, and 4.	

Beg toe inc:

4 dpn	5 dpn	2 circular needles
Rnd 1 Needle 1: K1, M1, knit to last st, M1, K1. Needle 2: K1, M1, knit to end. Needle 3: Knit to last st, M1, K1.	**Rnd 1** Needle 1: K1, M1, knit to end. Needle 2: Knit to last st, M1, K1. Needle 3: K1, M1, knit to end. Needle 4: Knit to last st, M1, K1.	**Rnd 1** Needle 1: K1, M1, knit to last st, M1, K1. Needle 2: K1, M1, knit to last st, M1, K1.

Rnd 2: Knit.
Rep rnds 1 and 2 until you have 48 (72, 96, 120) total sts.

Foot

Sl 1 st from needle 2 to needle 1. Work instep in patt on needle 1 with 25 (37, 49, 61) sts. Work sole in St st on needles 2 and 3 with 23 (35, 47, 59) sts.	Sl 1 st from needle 3 to needle 2. Work sole in St st on needles 3 and 4 with 23 (35, 47, 59) sts. Work instep in patt on needles 1 and 2 with 25 (37, 49, 61) sts.	Sl 1 st from needle 2 to needle 1. Work instep in patt on needle 1 with 25 (37, 49, 61) sts. Work sole in St st on needle 2 with 23 (35, 47, 59) sts.

Sts per needle:

(25, 11, 12), (37, 17, 18), (49, 23, 24), (61, 29, 30)	(12, 13, 11, 12), (18, 19, 17, 18), (24, 25, 23, 24), (30, 31, 29, 30)	(25, 23) (37, 35), (49, 47), (61, 59)

Beg each rnd of patt work with **extra st** on chart or in written instructions. This will balance patt over instep.

Beg working instep patt of choice on needle 1, and work in St st on needles 2 and 3 for sole.	Beg working instep patt of choice on needles 1 and 2, and work in St st on needles 3 and 4 for sole.	Beg working instep patt of choice on needle 1, and work in St st on needle 2 for sole.

Cont on 48 (72, 96, 120) sts to desired length of foot minus heel measurement. See charts on pages 13–14.

Heel

Work heel back and forth in rows on 23 (35, 47, 59) sts, beg on RS.
If sock needs extra durability, work heel flap on smaller needles or add reinforcing yarn to create firmer fabric.

Sl all sts from needle 2 to needle 3 for heel. Sl half sts from needle 1 to needle 2 to hold instep. Work heel on needle 3.	Sl heel sts from needle 4 to needle 3. Work heel on needle 3.	Work heel on needle 2.

Heel-bottom patt:
    Row 1 (RS): Knit to last st, sl as if to purl wyif.
    Row 2: K1, purl to last st, sl as if to purl wyif.
    Work in heel-bottom patt until you have 23 (35, 47, 59) heel-flap rows, ending with RS row, which is row 1.
Be sure to try your sock on. If your ankle is particularly deep, you may need to add additional heel-flap rows.

Heel Turn

Work heel st and cont up heel while working gusset.
    Row 1 (WS): Sl 1, P12 (18, 24, 30), P2tog, P1, turn.
    Row 2: Sl 1, K1, sl 1, K1, sl 1, ssk, K1, turn.
    Row 3: Sl 1, purl to within 1 st of gap, P2tog, P1, turn.
    Row 4: Sl 1, K2, *sl 1, K1, rep from * to within 1 st of gap, ssk, K1, turn.
    Row 5: Sl 1, purl to within 1 st of gap, P2tog, P1, turn.
    Row 6: Sl 1, *K1, sl 1, rep from * to within 1 st of gap, ssk, K1, turn.
    Rep rows 3, 4, 5, and 6, inc 1 additional knit or purl st after sl 1 until all side sts are worked, ending with RS (knit) row—13 (19, 25, 31) sts rem.

Heel Flap and Gusset

4 dpn	5 dpn	2 circular needles
Sl 6 (9, 12, 15) sts from RH side of heel sts to needle 4. LH needle is now needle 1. Sl all instep sts to needle 2.	Sl 6 (9, 12, 15) sts from RH side of heel sts to needle 5. LH needle is now needle 1. Instep sts are on needles 2 and 3.	Renumber needles; Needle 1: Heel sts Needle 2: Instep sts
Needle 1: PM before picking up sts, PU 12 (18, 24, 30) sts from heel flap, PU 2 extra sts at top of gusset (see page 25).		
Needle 2: Work instep in est patt. Needle 3: PU 2 sts at top of gusset, PU 12 (18, 24, 30) sts, PM, knit rem sts from heel turn.	Needles 2 and 3: Work instep in est patt. Needle 4: PU 2 sts at top of gusset, PU 12 (18, 24, 30) sts, PM, knit rem sts from heel turn.	Cont with needle 1: PM, work 13 (13, 25, 25) sts in est patt from needle 2 to needle 1. Needle 2: Work remaining 12, (24, 24, 36) instep sts in est patt, PM, PU 2 sts at top of gusset, PU 12 (18, 24, 30) sts, PM, K6 (9, 12, 15) from heel turn.
While working gusset, cont to work heel sts between markers as established on heel turn. Sts per needle:		
(21, 25, 20), (30, 37, 29), (39, 49, 38), (48, 61, 47)	(21, 13, 12, 20), (30, 13, 24, 29), (39, 25, 24, 38), (48, 25, 36, 47)	(34, 32), (43, 53), (64, 62), (73, 83)

Gusset Decrease and Heel-Back Patterning

As you look at work, you have 2 markers on sole/gusset. The heel st is worked only on center. For 2 circular needles, sts at beg of needle 1 and end of needle 2 are heel sts.

Work rnd 1 once to combine sts picked up and to eliminate gap at top of gusset.

4 dpn	5 dpn	2 circular needles
Rnd 1 Needle 1: Knit to last 2 sts, ssk. Needle 2: Work est patt. Needle 3: K2tog, knit to end.	**Rnd 1** Needle 1: Knit to last 2 sts, ssk. Needles 2 and 3: Work est patt. Needle 4: K2tog, knit to end.	Needle 1: Knit to last 2 sts before 2nd marker, ssk, SM, work est patt. Needle 2: Work est patt to first marker, SM, K2tog, knit to end.
Rnd 2 (dec rnd) Needle 1: *Sl 1, K1, rep from * to st before marker, sl 1, SM, knit to last 3 sts, K2tog, K1. Needle 2: Work est patt. Needle 3: K1, ssk, knit to marker, SM, *sl 1, K1, rep from * to end.	**Rnd 2 (dec rnd)** Needle 1: *Sl 1, K1, rep from * to st before marker, sl 1, SM, knit to last 3 sts, K2tog, K1. Needles 2 and 3: Work est patt. Needle 4: K1, ssk, knit to marker, SM, *sl 1, K1, rep from * to end.	**Rnd 2 (dec rnd)** Needle 1: *Sl 1, K1, rep from * to st before first marker, sl 1, SM, knit to last 3 sts before next marker, K2tog, K1, SM, work est patt to end. Needle 2: Work est patt to first marker, SM, ssk, K1, work to next marker, SM, *sl 1, K1, rep from * to end.
Rnd 3 Needle 1: Knit. Needle 2: Work est patt. Needle 3: Knit.	**Rnd 3** Needle 1: Knit. Needles 2 and 3: Work est patt. Needle 4: Knit.	**Rnd 3** Needle 1: Knit to 2nd marker, SM, work est patt. Needle 2: Work est patt to first marker, SM, knit to end.

Rep rnds 2 and 3 until 48 (72, 96, 120) total sts rem. Transfer sts as necessary so that patt rep begins on each
  needle.

Sts per needle:

(12, 24, 12), (24, 24, 24), (24, 36, 36), (36, 36, 48)	(12, 12, 12, 12), (12, 24, 12, 24), (24, 24, 24, 24), (24, 36, 24, 36)	24 (36, 48, 60)

Leg and Cuff

Beg with needle 1, work in patt around to desired leg length. (Remember to work just the 12 sts of the patt rep
  and *not* the extra st at beg of patt.)

Work K1, P1 ribbing for approximately 1½". BO loosely.

Round-Toe Cast On

*Note that for larger sizes, the number of plain rnds between inc rnds may make the toe too long. If you see this
  happening, knit fewer additional knit rows to obtain desired toe length.*

CO 8 sts and divide sts per needle as follows:

4 dpn	5 dpn	2 circular needles
2, 2, 4	2	4

Join into ring, being careful not to twist sts.

  Knit 1 rnd even.
  Inc rnd: K1f&b in each st—16 sts.
  Knit 1 rnd even.
  Next inc rnd: *K1, K1f&b, rep from * around—24 sts.
  Knit 2 rnds even.
  Next inc rnd: *K2, K1f&b, rep from * around—32 sts.
  Knit 3 rnds even.
  Next inc rnd: *K3, K1f&b, rep from * around—40 sts.
  Knit 4 rnds even.
  Cont in this manner, inc 1 more st between incs and knitting 1 more rnd in St st between incs to
  48 (72, 96, 120) total sts.

Sts per needle:

(12, 12, 24), (18, 18, 36), (24, 24, 48), (30, 30, 60)	12 (18, 24, 30)	24 (36, 48, 60)

Cont with "Foot" on page 59 for rem instructions.

Stitch Dictionary

Instructions are for working patterns in the round. All rows of charts are worked from right to left and from bottom to top. The written instructions begin with a stitch (indicated in brackets) and the charts begin with a separate column. This extra stitch is worked only once at the beginning of the instep. When working the leg, work only the 12-stitch repeats. The extra stitch has been added to balance the total pattern on the instep.

Fan Lace

Rnds 1, 3, 5, 7: [P1], *K11, P1, rep from *.

Rnd 2: [P1], *ssk, K1-b 3 times, YO, K1, YO, K1-b 3 times, K2tog, P1, rep from *.

Rnd 4: [P1], *ssk, K1-b twice, YO, K1, YO, ssk, YO, K1-b twice, K2tog, P1, rep from *.

Rnd 6: [P1], *ssk, K1-b, YO, K1, (YO, ssk) twice, YO, K1-b, K2tog, P1, rep from *.

Rnd 8: [P1], *ssk, YO, K1, (YO, ssk) 3 times, YO, K2tog, P1, rep from *.

Rep rnds 1–8.

Small Capitals

Rnd 1: [K1], *ssk, K3, YO, K1, YO, K3, K2tog, K1, rep from *.

Rnd 2: [K1], *ssk, K2, YO, K3, YO, K2, K2tog, K1, rep from *.

Rnd 3: [K1], *ssk, K1, YO, K5, YO, K1, K2tog, K1, rep from *.

Rnd 4: [K1], *ssk, YO, K7, YO, K2tog, K1, rep from *.

Rnd 5: [K1], *YO, K3, K2tog, K1, ssk, K3, YO, K1, rep from *.

Rnd 6: [K1], *K1, YO, K2, K2tog, K1, ssk, K2, YO, K2, rep from *.

Rnd 7: [K1], *K2, YO, K1, K2tog, K1, ssk, K1, YO, K3, rep from *.

Rnd 8: [K1], *K3, YO, K2tog, K1, ssk, YO, K4, rep from *.

Rep rnds 1–8.

Oriel

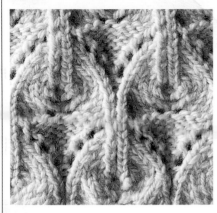

Rnds 1, 3, 5: [P1], *ssk, K3, YO, P1, YO, K3, K2tog, P1, rep from *.

Rnds 2, 4, 6, 8: [P1], *K5, P1, K5, P1, rep from *.

Rnd 7: [P1], *YO, K3, K2tog, P1, ssk, K3, YO, P1, rep from *.

Rnd 9: [P1], *P1, YO, K2, K2tog, P1, ssk, K2, YO, P2, rep from *.

Rnd 10: [P1], *P1, K4, P1, K4, P2, rep from *.

Rnd 11: [P1], *P2, YO, P1, K2tog, P1, ssk, K1, YO, P3, rep from *.

Rnd 12: [P1], *P2, K3, P1, K3, P3, rep from *.

Rnd 13: [P1], *P3, YO, K2tog, P1, ssk, YO, P4, rep from *.

Rnd 14: [P1], *P3, K2, P1, K2, P4, rep from *.

Rnds 15, 17, 19: [P1], *YO, K3, K2tog, P1, ssk, K3, YO, P1, rep from *.

Rnds 16, 18, 20, 22: [P1], *K5, P1, K5, P1, rep from *.

Rnd 21: [P1], *YO, K3, K2tog, P1, ssk, K3, YO, P1, rep from *.

Rnd 23: [P1], *ssk, K2, YO, P3, YO, K2, K2tog, P1, rep from *.

Rnd 24: [P1], *K4, P3, K4, P1, rep from *.

Rnd 25: [P1], *ssk, K1, YO, P5, YO, K1, ssk, P1, rep from *.

Rnd 26: [P1], *K3, P5, K3, P1, rep from *.

Rnd 27: [P1], *ssk, YO, P7, YO, K2tog, P1, rep from *.

Rnd 28: [P1], *K2, P7, K2, P1, rep from *.

Rep rnds 1–28.

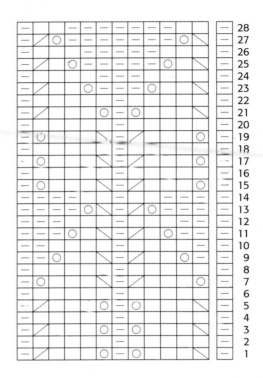

Cabled Patterns

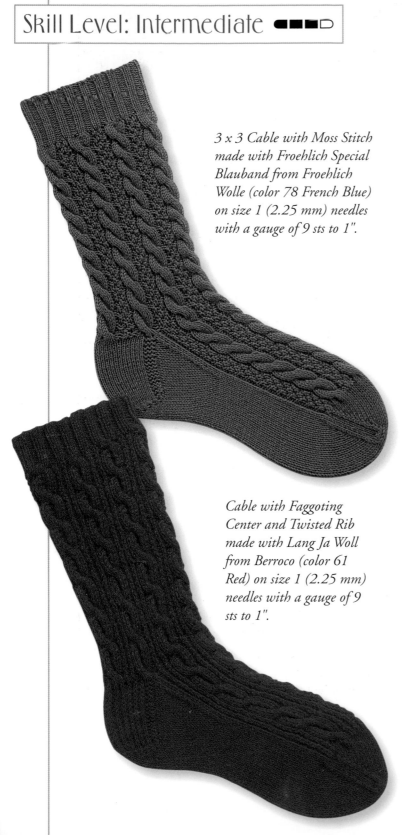

3 x 3 Cable with Moss Stitch made with Froehlich Special Blauband from Froehlich Wolle (color 78 French Blue) on size 1 (2.25 mm) needles with a gauge of 9 sts to 1".

Cable with Faggoting Center and Twisted Rib made with Lang Ja Woll from Berroco (color 61 Red) on size 1 (2.25 mm) needles with a gauge of 9 sts to 1".

The foundation of these socks is the 6-stitch cable, and many wonderful variations allow you to make the sock fancier. It's fun to change the cable patterns as well as the patterning between the cables for some variety. Cabled fabric is denser than plain pattern knitting and requires more yarn for a pair of socks. It's easier to work a complex pattern by keeping full-pattern repeats together. This pattern is easier to work with 4 double-pointed needles instead of 5. For this reason, instructions are provided only for 4 double-pointed needles and 2 circular needles.

Materials

Referring to "Sock Yarn" and "Sock Basics" on pages 8–17, gather materials for the socks you'd like to make.

Ring markers (for 2 circular needles technique)

Directions

Select the number of sts to CO based on the gauge for your yarn and needles and the circumference of the intended foot.

Stitch Table															
Foot Circumference in Inches															
Gauge Sts/1"	5	5½	6	6½	7	7½	8	8½	9	9½	10	10½	11	11½	12
Number of Stitches to CO															
5½							48	48							68
6						48							68	68	
6½					48						68	68			
7				48						68					
7½			48						68						
8								68							
8½		48					68								
9						68									
9½	48				68										
10				68											

When selecting size and yarn, remember that gauge is based only on St-st portion on sole of foot.

Cuff and Leg

Using long-tail CO method, CO 48 (68) sts. Divide sts per needle as follows:

4 dpn	2 circular needles
(16, 16, 16), (24, 24, 20)	24 (34)

Join, being careful not to twist sts, and work K2, P2 ribbing for 2".
Inc sts to 55 (77) as follows:
    For **48 sts:** K6, M1, (K6, M1) 6 times, K6.
    For **68 sts:** K7, M1, (K7, M1) 8 times, K6.
Divide sts per needle as follows:

(11, 22, 22), (22, 22, 33)	(22, 33), (33, 44)

Work cable patt to desired leg length, end by working 1 rnd after a cable cross.
Prepare for heel: Instep of sock has 2 (3) cables with decorative patt on either side of instep as well as between cables—total 27 (38) sts. The heel has 3 (4) cables with decorative sts between cables—total 28 (39) sts.

Sl 6 sts (the cable) from needle 2 to needle 3. Needle 3 holds sts for heel.	Sl 5 sts (patt between cable) from needle 2 to needle 1. Needle 2 holds sts for heel.
Sts per needle: (11, 16, 28), (22, 16, 39)	Sts per needle: (27, 28), (38, 39)

Heel Flap

Beg heel sts on WS row, working heel in St st with a garter panel on either side.

Row 1 (WS):

For 48 sts: P3, P2tog, (P3, P2tog) 4 times, P3—23 sts for heel flap.

For 68 sts: P3, P1, P2tog, (P4, P2tog) 5 times, P3—33 sts for heel flap.

Row 2: P3, purl to end.

Row 3: K3, knit to end.

For both sizes, rep rows 2 and 3 for 23 (33) more heel-flap rows, ending with RS row.

Variation: If you prefer, you can insert heel st for St st as follows:

Row 2 (RS): P3, *sl 1, K1, rep from * to last 4 sts, sl 1, K3.

Row 3: K3, purl to end.

Heel Turn

Row 1 (WS): Sl 1, P12 (17) sts, P2tog, P1, turn.

Row 2: Sl 1, K4, ssk, K1, turn.

Row 3: Sl 1, purl to within 1 st of gap, P2tog (1 st on either side of gap), P1, turn.

Row 4: Sl 1, knit to within 1 st of gap, ssk, K1, turn.

Rep rows 3 and 4, inc 1 additional knit or purl st after sl 1, until all side sts are worked; end with RS (knit) row—13 (19) sts left on heel flap.

Gusset

4 dpn	2 circular needles
Combine instep sts from needle 1 and 2 to needle 2. Sl 6 (9) sts to needle 4 from RH side of heel flap. Renumber needle 3 to needle 1. Needle 1 now has 7 (10) sts. Cont with needle 1, PU 11 (16) sts from side of heel flap, PU 2 extra sts at top of gusset (see page 25). Needle 2: Work 27 (38) instep sts in est cable patt. Needle 3: PU 2 extra sts at top of gusset, then PU 11 (16) from side of heel flap, K6 (9) from heel flap. Sts per needle: (20, 27, 19), (28, 38, 27)	Renumber needles as follows: Needle 1: Heel sts Needle 2: Instep sts With needle 1 (heel sts), PU 11 (16) sts from side of heel flap, PU 2 extra sts at top of gusset (see page 25), PM, from needle 2, work 16 (16) instep sts in cable patt. Needle 2: Work rem 11 (22) sts in cable patt from instep, PM, cont with needle 2, PU 2 extra sts at top of gusset, then PU 11 (16) sts from side of heel flap, K6 (9) from heel flap. Sts per needle: (36, 30), (44, 49)

Gusset Decrease

Work rnd 1 once to combine sts picked up and to eliminate gap at top of gusset.

Rnd 1	Rnd 1
Needle 1: Knit to last 2 sts, ssk. Needles 2 and 3: Work est patt. Needle 4: K2tog, knit to end.	Needle 1: Knit to 2 sts before marker, ssk, SM, work est patt to end to end. Needle 2: Work est patt to marker, SM, K2tog, knit to end.
Rnd 2 (dec rnd) Needle 1: Knit to last 3 sts, K2tog, K1. Needle 2: Work est patt. Needle 3: K1, ssk, knit to end.	**Rnd 2 (dec rnd)** Needle 1: Knit to last 3 sts before marker, K2tog, K1, SM, work est patt to end. Needle 2: Work est patt to marker, SM, K1, ssk, knit to end.

Rnd 3 Needle 1: Knit. Needle 2: Work est patt. Needle 3: Knit.	**Rnd 3** Needle 1: Knit to marker, SM, work est patt to end. Needle 2: Work est patt to marker, SM, knit to end.
Rep rnds 2 and 3 until total of 50 (71) sts rem. Sts per needle: (12, 27, 11), (17, 38, 16)	Rep rnds 2 and 3 until total of 50 (71) sts rem. Sts per needle: (28, 22), (33, 38) Rearrange sts so instep sts are on needle 1 and sole sts are on needle 2.

Foot

4 dpn	**2 circular needles**
Cont St st on needles 1 and 3 and patt on needle 2 to desired heel-to-toe length.	Cont patt on needle 1 and St st on needle 2 to desired heel-to-toe length.

Toe Shaping

Before working toe dec, you need to dec some sts from instep to create equal number of sts on instep and sole.

Instep Dec Rnd Needle 1: Knit. *For 48-st sock:* Needle 2: K4, K2tog, (K4, K2tog) 3 times, K3— 23 sts. *For 68-st sock:* Needle 2: K4, K2tog, (K5, K2tog) 4 times, K4— 33 sts.	**Instep Dec Rnd** *For 48-st sock:* Needle 1: K4, K2tog, (K4, K2tog) 3 times, K3— 23 sts. *For 68-st sock:* Needle 1: K4, K2tog, (K5, K2tog) 4 times, K4— 33 sts.
Renumber needles as follows:	
Needles 1 and 2: Sole sts Needle 3: Instep sts Sts per needle: (11, 12, 23), (16, 17, 33)	Needle 1: Sole sts Needle 2: Instep sts Sts per needle: 23 (33)
Rnd 1 Needle 1: K1, ssk, knit to end. Needle 2: Knit to last 3 sts, K2tog, K1. Needle 3: K1, ssk, knit to last 3 sts, K2tog, K1.	**Rnd 1** Needle 1: K1, ssk, knit to last 3 sts, K2tog, K1. Needle 2: K1, ssk, knit to last 3 sts, K2tog, K1.

Rnd 2: Knit around.

Rep rnds 1 and 2 until 22 (34) total sts rem.

Rep rnd 1 only until 14 (18) total sts rem.

Place sts from instep of sock on 1 needle and sts from bottom onto 2nd needle. Graft toe sts tog with kitchener st (see page 24).

Stitch Dictionary

Instructions are for working patterns in the round. All rows of charts are read and worked from right to left and from bottom to top.

3 x 3 Cable with Moss Stitch

Rnds 1, 2, 5, 6: *(P1, K1) twice, P1, K6, rep from *.

Rnds 3, 4: *P2, K1, P2, K6, rep from *.

Rnd 7: *P2, K1, P2, sl next 3 sts to cn and hold in front, K3, then K3 from cn, rep from *.

Rnd 8: *P2, K1, P2, K6, rep from *.

Rep rnds 1–8.

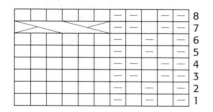

Picot Eyelet Cable with Seed Stitch

Rnds 1, 5, 7, 11, 15: *(P1, K1) twice, P1, K6, rep from *.

Rnds 2, 8, 12, 16: *(P2, K1) twice, K2tog, YO twice, ssk, K1, rep from *.

Rnds 3, 9, 13, 17: *(P1, K1) twice, P1, K2, P1, K3, rep from *.

Rnds 4, 10, 14: *P2, K1, P2, K6, rep from *.

Rnd 6: *P2, K1, P2, sl next 3 sts to cn and hold in front, K3, then K3 from cn, rep from *.

Rnd 18: *P2, K1, P2, K6, rep from *.

Rep rnds 1–18.

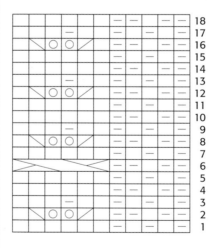

Cable with Faggoting Center and Twisted Rib

Rnds 1, 3, 5, 7, 9: *(P1, K1-b) twice, P1, K3, YO, K2tog, K1, rep from *.

Rnd 2: *(P1, K1) twice, P1, sl next 3 sts to cn and hold in front, K3, then K3 from cn, rep from *.

Rnds 4, 6, 8, 10: *(P1, K1) 3 times, ssk, YO, K3, rep from *.

Rep rnds 1–10.

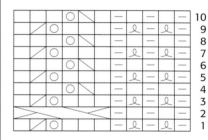

Open Cable with Twisted Rib

Rnds 1, 11: *P2, K1-b, P2, K6, rep from *.

Rnds 2, 4, 6, 8, 10, 12, 14, 16, 18: *P2, K1, P2, K6, rep from *.

Rnds 3, 13: *P2, K1-b, P2, sl next 3 sts to cn and hold in front, K3, then K3 from cn, rep from *.

Rnds 5, 7, 9: *P2, K1-b, P2, K4, YO, K2tog, rep from *.

Rnds 15, 17, 19: *P2, K1-b, P2, ssk, YO, K4, rep from *.

Rnd 20: *P2, K1, P2, K6, rep from *.

Rep rnds 1–20.

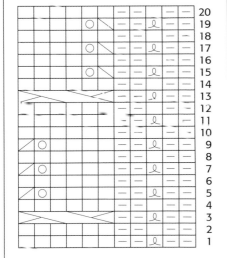

Waves and Footprints with Ladders

Rnds 1, 2, 6, 10: *P5, K6, rep from *.

Rnd 3: *K5, sl next 3 sts to cn and hold in front, K3, then K3 from cn, rep from *.

Rnds 4, 8: Knit.

Rnds 5, 9: *P5, K2, K2tog, YO, K2, rep from *.

Rnds 7, 11: *K7, YO, ssk, K2, rep from *.

Rnd 12: Knit.

Rep rnds 1–12.

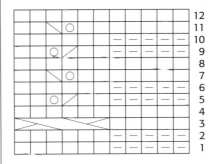

Braided Cable with Garter Bead

Rnds 1, 3, 5, 7, 9, 11: *P2, K1, P2, K6, rep from *.

Rnds 2, 6, 8: *P5, K6, rep from *.

Rnd 4: *P5, sl next 2 sts to cn and hold in front, K2, then K2 from cn, K2, rep from *.

Rnd 10: *P5, K2, sl next 2 sts to cn and hold in back, K2, then K2 from cn, rep from *.

Rnd 12: *P5, K6, rep from *.

Rep rnds 1–12.

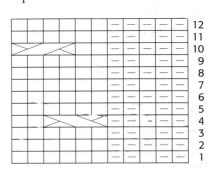

Chevron Patterns for Self-Striping Yarn

Skill Level: Intermediate ◼◼◼▭

Ridged Feather made with Magic Stripes from Lion Brand (color 204 Bright Spring Pattern) on size 3 (3.25 mm) needles with a gauge of 7 sts to 1".

Chevron made with Meilenweit Fun and Stripes from Lana Grossa (color 16) on size 1 (2.25 mm) needles with a gauge of 9 sts to 1".

Knitting self-striping yarn in chevron patterns creates a more visually interesting fabric than knitting these yarns in stockinette stitch. For this sock, I have invented the "forethought" heel, which is a slight variation of the "afterthought" heel. An afterthought heel is normally worked into a tube of knitting, a sock that was knit without any heel. The yarn is clipped and unraveled, and live stitches are picked up to work the afterthought heel. By working the classic afterthought heel structure before the foot, the sock is complete when you finish the toe. I feel that the forethought heel is easier and less trouble to work after knitting the cuff and leg than trying to do it after the toe is completed.

Materials

Referring to "Sock Yarn" and "Sock Basics" on pages 8–17, gather materials for the socks you'd like to make.

Small amount of waste yarn for provisional CO

Stitch holder

Directions

Select the number of sts to CO based on the gauge for your yarn and needles and the circumference of the intended foot.

Stitch Table														
Foot Circumference in Inches														
5	5½	6	6½	7	7½	8	8½	9	9½	10	10½	11	11½	12
Gauge Sts/1" — Number of Stitches to CO														
5½							44							66	
6						44							66		
6½					44						66	66			
7				44						66					
7½			44						66					88	88
8		44						66					88		
8½							66					88			
9	44								66		88				110
9½							66				88			110	
10				66					88				110		

Cuff and Leg

Using long-tail CO method, CO 44 (66, 88, 110) sts. Divide sts per needle as follows:

4 dpn	5 dpn	2 circular needles
(22, 11, 11), (33, 11, 22), (44, 22, 22), (55, 22, 33)	(11, 11, 11, 11), (11, 22, 11, 22), (22, 22, 22, 22), (22, 33, 22, 33)	22 (33, 44, 55)

Join, being careful not to twist sts. Work 3 ridges of garter st as follows:

    Rnds 1, 3, 5: Knit.

    Rnds 2, 4, 6: Purl.

Beg working patt of choice. Work leg to desired length, ending with complete patt rep. This places yarn ready to knit instep sts. This yarn will rest until heel is completed.

In-Place Afterthought or Forethought Heel

Needle 1: Instep sts Needles 2 and 3: Heel sts Sl instep sts from needle 1 to holder.	Needles 1 and 2: Instep sts Needles 3 and 4: Heel sts Sl instep sts from needle 1 and 2 to holder.	Needle 1: Instep sts Needle 2: Heel sts Sl instep sts from needle 1 to holder.

With scrap yarn, and needle 1, CO 22 (33, 44, 55) sts using the provisional CO (see page 22). Place needle 1 so that you're ready to knit CO sts instead of instep. Take yarn from other side of skein. Locate part of painted patt you're currently working in and start using that. The heel will cont in this patt and form concentric circles of patt, sometimes called "bull's-eye."

Preparation Round: Knit across these newly CO sts. Join with heel sts and knit across heel sts.

Sts on needles 2 and 3: (11, 11), (16, 17), (22, 22), (27, 28)	Sts on needles 2 and 3: (11, 11), (16, 17), (22, 22), (27, 28) (use 4 dpn to work heel)	Sts per needle: 22 (33, 44, 55)

Rnd 1	Rnd 1	Rnd 1
Needle 1 (provisional CO sts): K1, ssk, knit to last 3 sts, K2tog, K1. Needle 2 (half of heel sts): K1, ssk, knit to end. Needle 3 (half of heel sts): Knit to last 3 sts, K2tog, K1.	Needle 1 (provisional CO sts): K1, ssk, knit to last 3 sts, K2tog, K1. Needle 2 (half of heel sts): K1, ssk, knit to end. Needle 3 (half of heel sts): Knit to last 3 sts, K2tog, K1.	Needle 1 (needle with provisional CO): K1, ssk, knit to last 3 sts, K2tog, K1. Needle 2: K1, ssk, knit to last 3 sts, K2tog, K1.

Rnd 2: Knit around.

Work rnds 1 and 2 in St st until 16 (26, 32, 42) total sts rem. Graft sts tog with kitchener st (see page 24).

Foot

Using Needle 1, replace 22 (33, 44, 55) sts of instep that were placed on holder. Unzip provisional CO and PU 22 (33, 44, 55) sts. Many times you may only be able to PU 1 st fewer than you CO. If that is the case, just PU an extra st where it looks like you need one to avoid a gap.

Start rnd with instep sts. Sts per needle:

(22, 11, 11), (33, 11, 22), (44, 22, 22), (55, 22, 33) Needle 1: Instep sts Needles 2 and 3: Sole sts	(11, 11, 11, 11), (11, 22, 11, 22), (22, 22, 22, 22), (22, 33, 22, 33) Needles 1 and 2: Instep sts Needles 3 and 4: Sole sts	22 (33, 44, 55) Needle 1: Instep sts Needle 2: Sole sts

Rnd 1: (Instep) Start working instep of sock with patt where you left off (should be rnd 1 of patt) with sock yarn at instep.

    (Heel/sole): PU 2 sts in corner (see page 25). The extra 2 sts should be on heel needle. Knit across heel in St st. At next corner, PU 2 sts at heel to close gap, place these sts on heel needle as well. Cont working est patt on instep sts.

Rnd 2: (Instep) Work in est patt.

    (Sole): K2tog, knit across to last 2 sts, K2tog.

    Rep rnd 2 until 22 (33, 44, 55) total sts rem on heel. Cont est patt on instep and St st on sole to desired heel-to-toe length.

Toe Shaping

4 dpn	5 dpn	2 circular needles
Sts per needle:		
(22, 11, 11), (33, 11, 22), (44, 22, 22), (55, 22, 33)	(11, 11, 11, 11), (16, 17, 16, 17), (22, 22, 22, 22), (27, 28, 27, 28)	22 (33, 44, 55)
Rnd 1 Needle 1: K1, ssk, knit to last 3 sts, K2tog, K1. Needle 2: K1, ssk, knit to end. Needle 3: Knit to last 3 sts, K2tog, K1.	**Rnd 1** Needle 1: K1, ssk, knit to end. Needle 2: Knit to last 3 sts, K2tog, K1. Needle 3: K1, ssk, knit to end. Needle 4: Knit to last 3 sts, K2tog, K1.	**Rnd 1** Needle 1: K1, ssk, knit to last 3 sts, K2tog, K1. Needle 2: K1, ssk, knit to last 3 sts, K2tog, K1.

Rnd 2: Knit around.

Rep rnds 1 and 2 until 24 (34, 44, 54) total sts rem.

Rep rnd 1 only until 12 (18, 20, 26) total sts rem.

Place sts from top of sock on 1 needle and sts from bottom onto 2nd needle. Graft toe sts tog with kitchener st (see page 24).

Stitch Dictionary

Instructions are for working patterns in the round. All rows of charts are read and worked from right to left and from bottom to top.

Ridged Feather

Rnds 1, 2: Knit.
Rnd 3: *P2tog twice, YO, (K1, YO) 3 times, P2tog twice, rep from *.
Rnd 4: Knit.
Rep rnds 1–4.

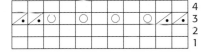

Chevron

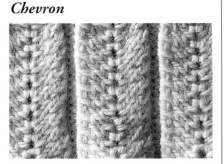

Rnd 1: *P2, K2tog, K2, (K1, YO, K1) in next st, K2, ssk, rep from *.
Rnd 2: *P2, K9, rep from *.
Rep rnds 1 and 2.

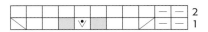

Welt Fantastic

Rnds 1, 3, 5, 7, 9, 11: Knit.
Rnds 2, 4: Purl.
Rnds 6, 8, 10, 12: *K2tog, K3, (K1, YO, K1) in next st, K3, ssk, rep from *.
Rep rnds 1–12.

Variations

The Chevron and Welt Fantastic patterns may be altered to make wider patterns, which will make the chevron peak more and give you more latitude in the number of stitches that can be cast on for a sock with an even number of pattern repeats. By adding 2 stitches to each repeat you now have a 13-stitch repeat; this is also a way to make the pattern more flexible for sizing. For instance, if you add 2 stitches to each repeat, instead of a 44-stitch sock, you'll now have a 52-stitch sock. At a gauge of 6½ stitches to the inch, the circumference would be 1¼" bigger. If you want to go larger, the next sock repeat would be 60 stitches.

Skill Level: Intermediate ◖◼◼◻▭

Burgundy, Natural, and Black (Pattern 2) made with Baby Ull from Dale of Norway (colors 4227 Burgundy, 0020 Natural, 0090 Black) on size 2 (2.75 mm) needles with a gauge of 8½ sts to 1".

Teal, Sage, and Peach (Pattern 5) made with Lang Ja Woll from Berroco (colors 88 Teal, 197 Sage, 175 Peach) on size 1 (2.25 mm) needles with a gauge of 9 sts to 1".

Some Fair Isle patterns are tessellated—where the dark and light patterns are identical. Working these patterns in 3 or more colors produces a lively and interesting fabric. This sock is designed with a short-row heel because it simplifies working the foot; there is no gusset or decrease. Work the heel, toe, and cuff in the same color for a calmer sock; work the cuff, heel, and toe in different colors for a livelier color combination.

Materials

Referring to "Sock Yarn" and "Sock Basics" on pages 8–17, gather materials for the socks you'd like to make. You will need 3 different colors of yarn for each pair of socks.

Ring markers or smooth, contrasting yarn for marking

Select the number of sts to CO based on the gauge for your yarn and needles and the circumference of the intended foot.

Stitch Table															
	Foot Circumference in Inches														
Gauge Sts/1"	5	5½	6	6½	7	7½	8	8½	9	9½	10	10½	11	11½	12
	Number of Stitches to CO														
5½			32			40		48			56			64	64
6		32		40	40		48		56	56		64	64		72
6½	32					48		56		64	64		72	72	80
7			40		48		56		64		72	72		80	
7½		40		48		56		64		72		80	80	88	88
8	40		48		56		64		72		80		88		96
8½		48		56		64		72		80		88	96	96	104
9					64		72		80		88	96		104	
9½	48		56			72		80		88	96		104	112	112
10		56		64	72		80		88	96		104	112		120

Cuff and Leg

The cuff, heel, and toe of the Burgundy, Natural, and Black sock were each knit with a different color. The cuff, heel, and toe of the Teal, Sage, and Yellow sock were knit with the same color.

Using long-tail CO and desired color, CO 32 (40, 48, 56, 64, 72, 80, 88, 96, 104, 112, 120) sts. Divide sts per needle as follows:

4 dpn	5 dpn	2 circular needles
(8, 8, 16), (10, 10, 20), (12, 12, 24), (14, 14, 28), (16, 16, 32), (18, 18, 36), (20, 20, 40), (22, 22, 44), (24, 24, 48), (26, 26, 52), (28, 28, 56), (30, 30, 60)	8 (10, 12, 14, 16, 18, 20, 22, 24, 26, 28, 30)	16 (20, 24, 28, 32, 36, 40, 44, 48, 52, 56, 60)

Join, being careful not to twist sts, and work K2, P2 ribbing for 1½". Change to patt of choice, work leg to desired length, ending with rnd of desired heel color before solid-colored rnd.

Short Row Heel

Work heel with heel yarn on 16 (20, 24, 28, 32, 36, 40, 44, 48, 52, 56, 60) sts.

Note that if you work heel sts with 3 needles (2 needles to hold heel and one to work sts), unworked sts are not stretched as much as if you use 2 needles. This also lessens the propensity to create gaps at base of heel.

Beg short-row shaping: The instructions include a lot of markers. They help when reversing short rows to keep things lined up. You can use ring markers or make your own. I used Knit Cro Sheen, but any smooth contrasting yarn will work fine. Cut short lengths and tie a knot to make a small ring.

Slip sts pwise unless otherwise instructed.

Row 1 (RS): K14 (18, 22, 26, 30, 34, 38, 42, 46, 50, 54, 58), yf, sl next st, yb, PM, sl wrapped st back to LH needle, turn.

Row 2: P12 (16, 20, 24, 28, 32, 36, 40, 44, 48, 52, 56), yb, sl next st, yf, PM, sl wrapped st back to LH needle, turn.

Row 3: Knit to st before last wrapped st, yf, sl next st, yb, PM, sl wrapped st back to LH needle, turn.

Row 4: Purl to st before last wrapped st, yb, sl next st, yf, PM, sl wrapped st back to LH needle, turn.

Rep rows 3 and 4 until 6 (8, 10, 12, 14, 14, 16, 18, 20, 20, 24, 24) sts rem unwrapped, end by working WS row.

Reverse short-row shaping. Note that your short rows will be more attractive if you sl the wrap up and over the st before knitting it tog with the st.

Row 1 (RS): Knit to next wrapped st, (1 st before marker) knit this st tog with wrap, remove marker, yf, sl next st, yb, sl wrapped st back to LH needle, turn. This st now has 2 wraps.

Row 2: Purl to next wrapped st, (1 st before marker) purl this st tog with wrap, remove marker, yb, sl next st to RH needle, yf, return st to LH needle, turn.

Row 3: Knit to next wrapped st (1 st before marker), sl knit st to RH needle, PU wraps with LH needle and place on RH needle, sl all 3 sts back to LH needle as if to purl, K3tog, remove marker, yf, sl next st, yb, sl st back to LH needle. Turn.

Row 4: Purl to next wrapped st (1 st before marker). Sl purl st kwise, PU 2 wraps from base of st and place on RH needle over first slipped st, sl them back one at a time pwise to LH needle, P3tog in back loop, remove marker, yb, sl next st pwise, yf, sl st back to LH needle, turn.

Rep rows 3 and 4 until you have worked all double wrapped sts, and removed all markers.

The 2 end sts have 1 wrap each. Beg knitting in rnd, with RS facing you. K14 (18, 22, 26, 30, 34, 38, 42, 46, 50, 54, 58) across heel until you reach last heel st with 1 wrap. Knit this st tog with its wrap.

Work across instep (this is solid-colored rnd in chart—we stopped just before here when working heel); when you get back to heel sts, knit first heel st tog with its wrap.

Foot

Cont working foot in est leg patt to desired heel-to-toe length; end by working solid-color rnd of desired toe color.

Toe Shaping for Star Toe

Work toe using 1 color only. Divide sts per needle as follows:

4 dpn	5 dpn	2 circular needles
(8, 8, 16), (10, 10, 20), (12, 12, 24), (14, 14, 28), (16, 16, 32), (18, 18, 36), (20, 20, 40), (22, 22, 44), (24, 24, 48), (26, 26, 52), (28, 28, 56), (30, 30, 60) On needle 3, pm after 8 (10, 12, 14, 16, 18, 20, 22, 24, 26, 28, 30) sts.	8 (10, 12, 14, 16, 18, 20, 22, 24, 26, 28, 30)	16 (20, 24, 28, 32, 36, 40, 44, 48, 52, 56, 60) On each needle, pm after 8 (10, 12, 14, 16, 18, 20, 22, 24, 26, 28, 30) sts.

Rnd 1: *Knit to last 2 sts on needle or before marker, K2tog, rep from *.
Rnd 2: Knit around.
Rep rnds 1 and 2 until 16 (20, 24, 28, 32, 36, 40, 44, 48, 52, 56, 60) total sts rem.
Rep rnd 1 only until 8 total sts rem. Break yarn and thread tail through the 8 sts and weave in on inside of sock.

Stitch Dictionary

Instructions are for working patterns in the round. All rows of charts are read and worked from right to left and from bottom to top.

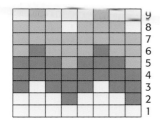

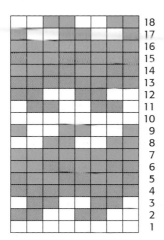

Pattern 1

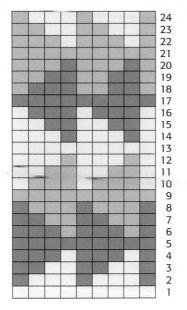

Pattern 3

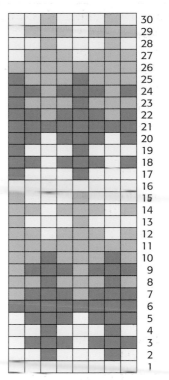

Pattern 5

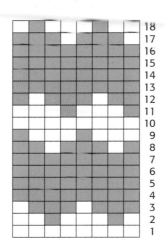

Pattern 2

Pattern 4

Four-Stitch Reticulated Patterns

Skill Level: Experienced ▪▪▪▪

Yellow and Blue (Pattern 1) made with Baby Ull from Dale of Norway (colors 2015 Yellow, 5545 Blue) on size 0 (2 mm) needles for cuff, and size 1 (2.25 mm) needles for body of sock, with a gauge of 10 sts = 1".

I have heard the word *reticulation* used to refer to an allover netlike pattern. I like the word and it's easier for me to think about one word than a phrase to describe these patterns.

This group of socks is knit using patterns that are 4 stitches wide. They are wonderful for socks because the patterns are easy to learn and, because the whole pattern is only 4 stitches wide, the longest possible float is only 3 stitches long. I happily allow those floats on my knitting with no problems. It's fun to use a hand-painted yarn for the pattern yarn. If you want to see the pattern clearly, it's best to choose a background yarn that is significantly darker than all the colors in the hand-painted yarn. Try a sample to make sure you like the look of the pattern before you begin. I've included a fun pattern Scandinavians traditionally call the "lice" pattern because of its tiny flecks.

Materials

Referring to "Sock Yarn" and "Sock Basics" on pages 8–17, gather materials for the socks you'd like to make. You will need 2 different colors of yarn for each pair of socks.

Ring markers (for 2 circular needles technique)

MC = cuff, heel, toe, and background pattern

CC = color pattern

Pine and Neon (Pattern 9) made with Shepherd Sock from Lorna's Laces (colors 20 Pine, 401 Neon) on size 0 (2 mm) needles for cuff ribbing, and size 1 (2.25 mm) needles for body of sock, with a gauge of 10 sts = 1".

Directions

Select the number of sts to CO based on the gauge for your yarn and needles and the circumference of the intended foot.

Stitch Table

Gauge Sts/1"	Foot Circumference in Inches														
	5	5½	6	6½	7	7½	8	8½	9	9½	10	10½	11	11½	12
	Number of Stitches to CO														
5½			32			40		48			56			64	64
6		32		40	40	48		56	56			64	64		72
6½	32				48			56		64	64		72	72	80
7			40		48		56		64		72	72	80		
7½		40		48		56		64		72		80	80	88	88
8	40		48		56		64		72		80		88		96
8½		48		56		64		72		80		88	96	96	104
9					64		72		80		88	96		104	
9½	48		56			72		80		88	96		104	112	112
10		56		64	72		80		88	96		104	112		120

Cuff and Leg

Using long-tail CO method and MC, CO 32 (40, 48, 56, 64, 72, 80, 88, 96, 104, 112, 120) sts.
Divide sts per needle as follows:

4 dpn	5 dpn	2 circular needles
(8, 8, 16), (10, 10, 20), (12, 12, 24), (14, 14, 28), (16, 16, 32), (18, 18, 36), (20, 20, 40), (22, 22, 44), (24, 24, 48), (26, 26, 52), (28, 28, 56), (30, 30, 60)	8 (10, 12, 14, 16, 18, 20, 22, 24, 26, 28, 30)	16 (20, 24, 28, 32, 36, 40, 44, 48, 52, 56, 60)

Join, being careful not to twist sts. Work K2, P2 ribbing for 1½". Change to patt of choice. Knit 1 rnd with MC. Change to larger needles and beg with needle 1, work patt in 2-color stranded knitting with MC and CC. Knit to desired leg length; end by working a complete rep of patt or a pleasing spot to have leg patt meet heel.

Heel Flap

The heel is worked back and forth in rows on 15 (19, 23, 27, 31, 35, 39, 43, 47, 51, 55, 59) sts.
Work Eye of Partridge heel in 2 colors with garter-st edges. Beg on a WS row to have both yarns available for heel without breaking yarn.

Sl 1 st from needle 3 to needle 2. Needles 1 and 2: Instep sts Needle 3: Heel sts	Sl 1 st from needle 4 to needle 1, slip all the sts from needle 4 to needle 3. Set needle 4 aside. Needles 1 and 2: Instep sts Needle 3: Heel sts	Sl 1 st from needle 2 to needle 1. Needle 1: Instep sts Needle 2: Heel sts

Sts per needle:		
(8, 9, 15), (10, 11, 19), (12, 13, 23), (14, 15, 27), (16, 17, 31), (18, 19, 35), (20, 21, 39), (22, 23, 43), (24, 25, 47), (26, 27, 51), (28, 29, 55), (30, 31, 59)	(8, 9, 15), (10, 11, 19), (12, 13, 23), (14, 15, 27), (16, 17, 31), (18, 19, 35), (20, 21, 39), (22, 23, 43), (24, 25, 47), (26, 27, 51), (28, 29, 55), (30, 31, 59)	(17, 15), (21, 19), (25, 23), (29, 27), (33, 31), (37, 35), (41, 39), (45, 43), (49, 47), (53, 51), (57, 55), (61, 59)

Turn work to beg a WS row across heel needle. In working this heel, RS rows are knit with MC only and slipping CC sts, and WS rows are worked in 2-color stranded purl sts.

Eye of Partridge heel st;

Row 1 (WS): K3 with MC, *P1 with MC, P1 with CC, rep from * to last 4 sts, P1 with MC, P3 with MC.

Row 2 (RS): With MC, P3, *K1, sl 1 wyib, rep from * across, weaving in slipped color across to last 4 sts, K4.

Row 3: K3 with MC, *P1 with CC, P1 with MC, rep from * to last 4 sts, P1 with CC, P3 with MC.

Row 4: With MC, P3, *sl 1 wyib, K1, rep from * across, weaving in slipped color across to last 4 sts; sl 1, K3.

Working heel with Eye of Partridge st in 2 colors creates a longer heel flap than one worked in 1 color. Measure for appropriate length from a pair of socks that fit or from measurement in foot-size charts on pages 13–14. End by working a RS (knit) row.

Heel Turn

First row of heel turn is WS row.

Work heel turn with MC only.

Row 1 (WS): Sl 1, P8 (10, 12, 14, 16, 18, 20, 22, 24, 26, 28, 30), P2tog, P1, turn.

Row 2: Sl 1 wyib, K4, ssk, K1, turn.

Row 3: Sl 1 wyib, purl to within 1 st of gap, P2tog (1 st on either side of gap), P1, turn.

Row 4: Sl 1 wyib, knit to within 1 st of gap, ssk, K1, turn.

Rep rows 3 and 4, inc 1 additional knit or purl st after sl 1 until side sts are worked, ending with RS (knit) row—9 (11, 13, 15, 17, 19, 21, 23, 25, 27, 29, 31) sts left on heel flap.

Gusset

4 dpn	5 dpn	2 circular needles
Divide heel sts onto needle 1 and needle 4, placing half minus 1 st on needle 1. Sts on needles 1 and 4: (4, 5), (5, 6), (6, 7), (7, 8), (8, 9), (9, 10), (10, 11), (11, 12), (12, 13), (13, 14), (14, 15), (15, 16). Needle 2: Instep sts	Divide heel sts onto needle 1 and needle 5, placing half minus 1 st on needle 1. Sts on needles 1 and 5: (4, 5), (5, 6), (6, 7), (7, 8), (8, 9), (9, 10), (10, 11), (11, 12), (12, 13), (13, 14), (14, 15), (15, 16). Needles 2 and 3: Instep sts	Renumber needles as follows: Needle 1: Heel sts Needle 2: Instep sts

With needle 1, PU sts along side of heel flap with MC, weaving in CC as you work your way up, so that CC will be there when you need to start working instep. (Or cut CC and reattach CC to start working instep.) Cont with needle 1, PU 2 extra sts at top of gusset (see page 25).

Needle 2: Work across instep, resuming place in chart. Needle 3: With MC, PU 2 sts at top of gusset.	With needles 2 and 3, work across instep, resuming place in chart. Needle 4: With MC, PU 2 sts at top of gusset.	Cont with needle 1: PM, work across 9 (11, 13, 15, 17, 19, 21, 23, 25, 27, 29, 31) instep sts, resuming place in chart. Needle 2: Work rem instep sts, PM, PU 2 extra sts at top of gusset with MC.

Cont with needle in hand, PU sts on side of heel flap in lice patt as follows: *3 sts with MC, 1 st with CC, rep from * until you have picked up all sts on side of gusset.

Work sole in lice patt (see chart on page 82). Cont in patt from picking up gusset sts.

4 dpn	5 dpn	2 circular needles
Work 5 (6, 7, 8, 9, 10, 11, 12, 13, 14, 15, 16) sts from heel flap in lice patt from spare needle.	Work 5 (6, 7, 8, 9, 10, 11, 12, 13, 14, 15, 16) sts from heel flap in lice patt from spare needle.	Work 5 (6, 7, 8, 9, 10, 11, 12, 13, 14, 15, 16) sts from heel flap in lice patt from needle 1 to needle 2.

Beg of rnd is now at center bottom of sock for shaping and at side of foot for color work; this eliminates any color jog in foot portion of sock.

Gusset Decrease

Work rnd 1 once to combine sts picked up and to eliminate gap at top of gusset.

Rnd 1 Needle 1: Work lice patt to last 2 sts, ssk with MC. Needle 2: Work est patt. Needle 3: K2tog with MC, work lice patt to end.	**Rnd 1** Needle 1: Work lice patt to last 2 sts, ssk with MC. Needles 2 and 3: Work est patt. Needle 4: K2tog with MC, work lice patt to end.	**Rnd 1** Needle 1: Work lice patt to last 2 sts before marker, ssk with MC, SM, work est patt to end. Needle 2: Work est patt to marker, SM, K2tog with MC, work lice patt to end.
Rnd 2 (dec rnd) Needle 1: Work lice patt to last 3 sts, K2tog with CC, K1 with MC. Needle 2: Work est patt. Needle 3: K1 with MC, ssk with CC, work lice patt.	**Rnd 2 (dec rnd)** Needle 1: Work lice patt to last 3 sts, K2tog with CC, K1 with MC. Needles 2 and 3: Work est patt. Needle 4: K1 with MC, ssk with CC, work lice patt to end.	**Rnd 2 (dec rnd)** Needle 1: Work lice patt to last 3 sts before marker, K2tog with CC, K1 with MC, SM, work est patt to end. Needle 2: Work est patt to marker, SM, K1 with MC, ssk with CC, work lice patt to end.
Rnd 3 Needle 1: Work lice patt. Needle 2: Work est patt. Needle 3: Work lice patt.	**Rnd 3** Needle 1: Work lice patt. Needles 2 and 3: Work est patt. Needle 4: Work lice patt.	**Rnd 3** Needle 1: Work lice patt to marker, SM, work est patt to end. Needle 2: Work est patt to marker, SM, work lice patt to end.

Rep rnds 2 and 3 until 32 (40, 48, 56, 64, 72, 80, 88, 96, 104, 112, 120) total sts rem.

Foot

Cont leg/instep patt on needle 2, and lice patt on needles 3 and 1 to desired heel-to-toe length.	Cont leg/instep patt on needles 2 and 3, and lice patt on needles 4 and 1 to desired heel-to-toe length.	Rearrange sts so all instep sts are on needle 1, and sole sts are on needle 2. Cont leg/instep patt on needle 1, and lice patt on needle 2 to desired heel-to-toe length.

Work 1 rnd in MC, drop CC and rearrange sts so extra st that was moved from heel/sole is put back on instep and you have same number of sts on instep as you do on sole.

Sts per needle:

(8, 16, 8), (10, 20, 10), (12, 24, 12), (14, 28, 14), (16, 32, 16), (18, 36, 18), (20, 40, 20), (22, 44, 22), (24, 48, 24), (26, 52, 26), (28, 56, 28), (30, 60, 30)	8 (10, 12, 14, 16, 18, 20, 22, 24, 26, 28, 30)	16 (20, 24, 28, 32, 36, 40, 44, 48, 52, 56, 60)

Toe Shaping

Change to smaller needle size. Beg of rnd is now at side of sock. Toe is knit using MC only.

4 dpn	5 dpn	2 circular needles
Knit sts on needle 1. Beg of rnd now shifts to side of foot that is ready to work instep. **Rnd 1** Needle 1: K1, ssk, knit to last 3 sts, K2tog, K1. Needle 2: K1, ssk, knit to end. Needle 3: Knit to last 3 sts, K2tog, K1.	Knit sts on needle 1. Beg of rnd now shifts to side of foot that is ready to work instep. **Rnd 1** Needle 1: K1, ssk, knit to end. Needle 2: Knit to last 3 sts, K2tog, K1. Needle 3: K1, ssk, knit to end. Needle 4: Knit to last 3 sts, K2tog, K1.	**Rnd 1** Needle 1: K1, ssk, knit to last 3 sts, K2tog, K1. Needle 2: K1, ssk, knit to last 3 sts, K2tog, K1.

Rnd 2: Knit around.

Rep rnds 1 and 2 until 16 (20, 24, 28, 32, 36, 40, 44, 48, 52, 56, 60) total sts rem.

Work rnd 1 only until 8 (8, 12, 12, 12, 12, 16, 16, 16, 20, 20, 20) total sts rem.

Place sts from top of sock on 1 needle and sts from bottom onto 2nd needle. Graft toe sts tog with kitchener st (see page 24).

Stitch Dictionary

Instructions are for working patterns in the round. All rows of charts are worked from right to left and from bottom to top.

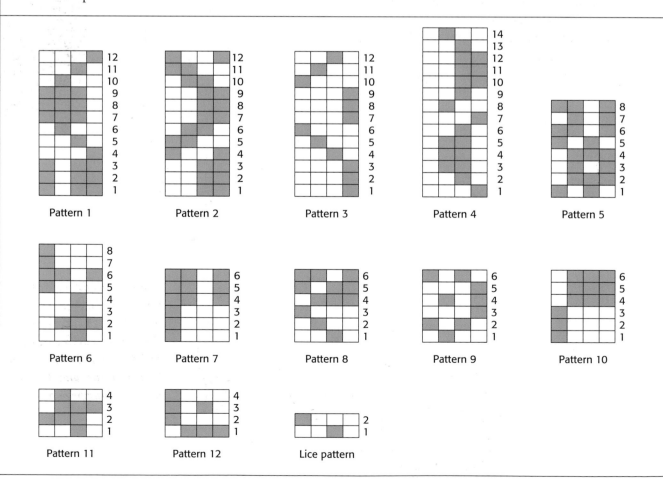

Pattern 1 Pattern 2 Pattern 3 Pattern 4 Pattern 5

Pattern 6 Pattern 7 Pattern 8 Pattern 9 Pattern 10

Pattern 11 Pattern 12 Lice pattern

Mosaic Patterns

Mosaic patterns are *magical*. You work with only 1 yarn at a time for 2 rounds, and after a few rounds, a lovely complex pattern emerges. You can choose to work the pattern as a garter-stitch fabric (knit the first round and purl the second) or as a stockinette-stitch fabric (knit every round). Either way, these are certainly distinctive socks. Using hand-painted yarn makes for lots of visual interest without any more work. You also have the option of working the heel and foot in a solid color.

Materials

Referring to "Sock Yarn" and "Sock Basics" on pages 8–17, gather materials for the socks you'd like to make. You will need 1 dark and 1 light yarn for each pair of socks.

Ring markers (for 2 circular needles technique)

Caesar's Check made with Shepherd Sock from Lorna's Laces (colors 16 Charcoal, 92 River) on size 1 needles with a gauge of 9½ sts to 1".

Maze made with Gems Opal from Louet Sales (colors 56 Navy, 01 Champagne) on size 2 needles with a gauge of 7½ sts to 1" in single color St st or mosaic, and 8½ sts to 1" in pinstripe patt.

Directions

Select the number of sts to CO based on the gauge for your yarn and needles and the circumference of the intended foot.

Stitch Table															
Gauge Sts/1"	**Foot Circumference in Inches**														
	5	5½	6	6½	7	7½	8	8½	9	9½	10	10½	11	11½	12
	Number of Stitches to CO														
5½	28					42	42				56	56			
6					42				56	56					
6½				42				56				70	70		
7			42				56				70			84	84
7½		42				56				70			84		
8					56			70	70			84			98
8½	42			56							84			98	
9							70			84			98		112
9½			56			70			84			98		112	
10		56			70			84			98		112		

Caesar's Check Sock

The leg of this sock is worked in Caesar's Check patt, a garter-stitch-based patt, which requires working every other rnd in purl. It's a denser fabric but results in a more textured fabric. The foot is worked in a loose rib that cont the stripe sequence of the leg.

Cuff and Leg

Using long-tail CO and dark, CO 28 (42, 56, 70, 84, 98, 112) sts. Divide sts per needle as follows:

4 dpn	5 dpn	2 circular needles
(7, 7, 14), (7, 14, 21), (14, 14, 28), (14, 21, 35), (21, 21, 42), (21, 28, 49), (28, 28, 56)	(7, 7, 7, 7), (7, 14, 7, 14), (14, 14, 14, 14), (14, 21, 14, 21), (21, 21, 21, 21), (21, 28, 21, 28), (28, 28, 28, 28)	14 (21, 28, 35, 42, 49, 56)

Join, being careful not to twist sts, and work K1, P1 ribbing for 1½".

Knit 1 rnd with dark. Beg working patt of choice, adding light. Work to desired length; end by working a complete patt rep or at an attractive place at top of heel.

Heel Flap

Heel is worked back and forth in rows on 14 (20, 28, 34, 42, 48, 56) sts, beg with WS row and ending with RS row.

Rearrange sts to work heel as follows:		
Sl 0 (1, 0, 1, 0, 1, 0) sts from needle 3 to needle 1. Sts per needle: (7, 7, 14), (8, 14, 20), (14, 14, 28), (15, 21, 34), (21, 21, 42), (22, 28, 48), (28, 28, 56) Work heel sts on needle 3.	Sl all sts from needle 4 to needle 3. Set needle 4 aside until gusset. Move 0, (1, 0, 1, 0, 1, 0) sts from needle 3 to needle 1. Sts per needle: (7, 7, 14), (8, 14, 20), (14, 14, 28), (15, 21, 34), (21, 21, 42), (22, 28, 48), (28, 28, 56) Work heel sts on needle 3.	Sl 0, (1, 0, 1, 0, 1, 0) sts from needle 2 to needle 1. Sts per needle: (14, 14), (22, 20), (28, 28), (36, 34), (42, 42), (50, 48), (56, 56) Work heel sts on needle 2.

Heel-st patt:

Beg heel with dark even if you just finished using that color in patt.

Working heel-st patt in 2 colors produces a heel flap that is much longer than one that is worked on same number of rows using only 1 color. Don't work this heel by counting rows. Measure a pair of socks that fit, measure your foot, or use heel-flap length from size charts on pages 13–14.

Work rows 1 and 2 with dark only.

Row 1 (WS): K3, purl to end.

Row 2: P3, *K1, sl 1, rep to last 3 sts, K3.

Work rows 3 and 4 with dark and light.

Row 3: K3 with light, *P1 with dark, P1 with light, rep from * to last 4 sts, P1 with dark, P3 with light.

Row 4: K3 with light, *sl 1, K1 with light, rep from *, weaving in slipped color across to last 4 sts, sl 1, K3 with light.

Rep rows 3 and 4 to desired heel length, ending with completed RS row.

Heel Turn

Row 1 (WS): With dark, sl 1, P7 (10, 14, 17, 21, 24, 28), P2 tog, P1, turn.

Row 2: Sl 1, K3, ssk, K1, turn.

Row 3: Sl 1, purl to within 1 st of gap, P2tog (1 st on either side of gap), P1, turn.

Row 4: Sl 1, knit to within 1 st of gap, ssk, K1, turn.

Rep rows 3 and 4, inc 1 additional knit or purl st after sl 1 until all side sts are worked, end with knit row—10 (12, 16, 20, 24, 26, 30) sts rem on heel flap.

4 dpn	5 dpn	2 circular needles
Sl half of heel sts to needle 4. Sts on left hand of heel are now needle 1.	Sl half of heel sts to needle 5. Sts on left hand of heel are now needle 1.	Renumber needles as follows: Needle 1: Heel sts Needle 2: Instep sts

Gusset

Needle 1: With dark, PU 1 st for each garter bump from side of heel flap, then PU 2 extra sts at top of gusset.

Needle 2 for sizes 28, 56, 84, 112: *P1, K5, P1, rep from *. Needle 2 for sizes 42, 70, 98: K2, *P2, K5, rep from * end P2, K2. Needle 3: PU 2 sts at top of gusset (see page 25), then 1 st for each garter bump. Knit rem heel sts.	Needles 2 and 3 for sizes 28, 56, 84, 112: *P1, K5, P1, rep from *. Needles 2 and 3 for sizes 42, 70, 98: K2, *P2, K5, rep from * end P2, K2. Needle 4: PU 2 sts at top of gusset (see page 25), then 1 st for each garter bump. Knit rem heel sts.	Cont with needle 1, PM, for sizes 28, 56, 84, and 112, *P1, K5, P1, rep from *. For sizes 42, 70, and 98, K2, *P2, K5, rep from * end P2, K2. Needle 2: Cont in instep rib patt for 7 (11, 14, 18, 21, 25, 28) sts, PM, PU 2 sts at top of gusset (see page 25), then 1 st for each garter bump, K5 (6, 8, 10, 12, 13, 15) heel sts.

Gusset Decrease

Work foot patt as follows: 2 rnds with light and 2 rnds with dark.

Work rnd 1 once to combine sts picked up and to eliminate gap at top of gusset.

4 dpn	5 dpn	2 circular needles
Rnd 1 Needle 1: Knit to last 2 sts, ssk. Needle 2: Work est rib patt. Needle 3: K2tog, knit to end.	**Rnd 1** Needle 1: Knit to last 2 sts, ssk. Needles 2 and 3: Work est rib patt. Needle 4: K2tog, knit to end.	**Rnd 1** Needle 1: Knit to last 2 sts before marker, ssk, SM, work est rib patt. Needle 2: Work est rib patt to marker, SM, K2tog, knit to end.
Rnd 2 (dec rnd) Needle 1: Knit to last 3 sts, K2tog, K1. Needle 2: Work est rib patt. Needle 3: K1, ssk, knit around.	**Rnd 2 (dec rnd)** Needle 1: Knit to last 3 sts, K2tog, K1. Needles 2 and 3: Work est rib patt. Needle 4: K1, ssk, knit around.	**Rnd 2 (dec rnd)** Needle 1: Knit to last 3 sts before marker, K2tog, K1, SM, work est rib patt. Needle 2: Work est patt, SM, K1, ssk, knit around.
Rnd 3 Needle 1: Knit. Needle 2: Work est rib patt. Needle 3: Knit.	**Rnd 3** Needle 1: Knit. Needles 2 and 3: Work est rib patt. Needle 4: Knit.	**Rnd 3** Needle 1: Knit to marker, SM, work est rib patt. Needle 2: Work est rib patt to marker, SM, knit to end.

Rep rnds 2 and 3 until 28 (44, 56, 72, 84, 100, 112) total sts rem.

Foot

Cont St st on needles 1 and 3, and est patt on needle 2, to desired heel-to-toe length.	Cont St st on needles 1 and 4, and est patt on needles 2 and 3, to desired heel-to-toe length.	Rearrange sts so that all instep sts are on needle 1, and all sole sts are on needle 2. Cont est patt on needle 1 and St st on needle 1 to desired heel-to-toe length.

Cont working St st on sole and in est patt on instep to desired heel-to-toe length; end by working 2 rnds of dark.

Toe Shaping for Round Toe

Note that the round toe takes 28 rnds to complete. The standard toe takes 7 (12, 17, 20, 25, 30, 35) rnds. This toe is most appropriate for a sock with 70, 84, 98 sts. For smaller sizes the round toe would be too long and for larger sizes not long enough.

With light, work dec/inc rnds as appropriate for size:

  28 sts: (K5, K2tog) 4 times—24 sts.
  42 sts: (K19, K2tog) twice—40 sts.
  56 sts: Knit around without dec.
  70 sts: K7, K2tog, (K9, K2tog) 5 times, K6—64 sts.
  84 sts: (K19, K2tog) 4 times—80 sts.
  98 sts: (K47, K2tog) twice—96 sts.
  112 sts: Knit around without dec.
Work toe on 24 (40, 56, 72, 80, 96, 112) sts.

Round-Toe Shaping (Or see below for alternate "Standard-Toe Shaping.")

Toes are worked in a different stripe sequence.

With light

First dec rnd: *K6, K2tog, rep from *.

Change to dark

Knit 6 rnds.

2nd dec rnd: *K5, K2tog, rep from *.

Change to light

Knit 5 rnds.

3rd dec rnd: *K4, K2tog, rep from *.

Change to dark

Knit 4 rnds.

4th dec rnd: *K3, K2tog, rep from *.

Change to light

Knit 3 rnds.

5th dec rnd: *K2, K2tog, rep from *.

Change to dark

Knit 2 rnds.

6th dec rnd: *K1, K2tog, rep from *.

Change to light

Knit 1 rnd.

7th dec rnd: K2tog around.

Cut yarn, leaving 12" tail. Thread tail onto darning needle and pull through rem sts firmly.

Standard-Toe Shaping

Cont with 2 rnds of dark and 2 rnds of light as est on foot.

4 dpn	5 dpn	2 circular needles
Knit sts on needle 1. Beg of rnd has shifted; renumber needles. For toe instructions, instep sts will now be on needle 1, and sole sts on needles 2 and 3	Knit sts on needle 1. Beg of rnd has shifted; renumber needles. For toe instructions, instep sts will now be on needles 1 and 2, and sole sts on needles 3 and 4.	Rnd 1 Needle 1: K1, ssk, knit to last 3 sts, K2tog, K1. Needle 2: K1, ssk, knit to last 3 sts, K2tog, K1.
Rnd 1 Needle 1: K1 ssk, knit to last 3 sts, K2tog, K1. Needle 2: K1, ssk, knit to end. Needle 3: Knit to last 3 sts, K2tog, K1.	Rnd 1 Needle 1: K1, ssk, knit to end. Needle 2: Knit to last 3 sts, K2tog, K1. Needle 3: K1, ssk, knit to end. Needle 4: Knit to last 3 sts, K2tog, K1.	

Rnd 2: Knit around.

Rep rnds 1 and 2 until 12 (20, 28, 36, 40, 48, 56) total sts rem.

Rep rnd 1 only until 8 (12, 16, 20, 20, 24, 28) total sts rem.

Place sts from top of sock on 1 needle and sts from bottom onto 2nd needle. Graft toe sts tog with kitchener st (see page 24).

Maze Sock

The leg of this sock is worked in Maze patt, which is a St-st-based patt. The foot is worked in St st with Fair Isle pinstripe patt.

Cuff and Leg

Using long-tail CO and dark, CO 28 (42, 56, 70, 84, 98, 112) sts. Divide sts per needle as follows:

4 dpn	5 dpn	2 circular needles
(7, 7, 14), (7, 14, 21), (14, 14, 28), (14, 21, 35), (21, 21, 42), (21, 28, 49), (28, 28, 56)	(7, 7, 7, 7), (7, 14, 7, 14), (14, 14, 14, 14), (14, 21, 14, 21), (21, 21, 21, 21), (21, 28, 21, 28), (28, 28, 28, 28)	14 (21, 28, 35, 42, 49, 56)

Join, being careful not to twist sts, and work K1, P1 ribbing for 1½".

Knit 1 rnd with dark. Beg working patt of choice, adding light. Cont to desired leg length; end by working rnd 15 or 31, or work only first of 2 rnds of last rep. This will allow you to work instep sts of gusset, pick up rnd with only 1 color, and then beg color work on first rnd after all sts are picked up. Stick with me—it will be easier later.

Heel Flap

Use dark for heel and heel turn.

Heel is worked back and forth in rows on 14 (20, 28, 34, 42, 48, 56) sts, starting on WS row, and end heel turn by working RS row.

Rearrange sts for heel as follows:

Sl 0 (1, 0, 1, 0, 1, 0) sts from needle 3 to needle 1. Work heel on needle 3.	Sl 0 (1, 0, 1, 0, 1, 0) sts from needle 4 to needle 1. Sl all sts from needle 4 to needle 3 to work heel. Work heel on needle 3.	Sl 0 (1, 0, 1, 0, 1, 0) sts from needle 2 to needle 1. Work heel on needle 2.

Heel-st patt:

  Row 1 (WS): K3, purl to end of row.
  Row 2: P3, *K1, sl 1, rep to last 3 sts, K3.
  Rep rows 1 and 2 for 14 (20, 28, 34, 42, 48, 56) total rows in heel flap, ending with RS row.

Heel Turn

  Row 1 (WS): P9 (12, 16, 19, 23, 26, 30) sts, P2tog, P1, turn.
  Row 2: Sl 1, K5, ssk, K1, turn.
  Row 3: Sl 1, purl to within 1 st of gap, P2tog (1 st on either side of gap), P1, turn.
  Row 4: Sl 1, knit to within 1 st of gap, ssk, K1, turn.
  Rep rows 3 and 4, inc 1 additional knit or purl st after sl 1 until all side sts are worked, ending with RS (knit) row—10 (12, 16, 20, 24, 26, 30) sts left on heel flap.

Gusset

Sl half of heel sts to needle 4; heel sts are now on needles 1 and 4.	Sl half of heel sts to needle 5; heel sts are now on needles 1 and 5.	Renumber needles as follows: Needle 1: Heel sts Needle 2: Instep sts

To work Fair Isle pinstripe patt, the entire PU round is worked in dark only and then the first gusset dec rnd is worked in dark as far as instep where you beg working Pinstripe patt with both dark and light. When you get to instep, light is there ready to beg patt. Work pinstripe patt as follows: K1 with dark, K1 with light. When you get to sole/gusset dec, cont with est pinstripe patt from instep. Make sure to always dec in same color (knit each dark st with dark, and each light st with light); this will produce an uninterrupted line along foot.

With dark and needle 1: PU 7 (10, 14, 17, 21, 24, 28) sts from side of heel flap, then PU 2 sts at top of gusset (see page 25).		
Needle 2: With dark, work 2nd rnd of last rep of Maze patt. Needle 3: PU 2 sts at top of gusset and 7 (10, 14, 17, 21, 24, 28) sts from side of heel flap, knit rem heel sts.	Needles 2 and 3: With dark, work 2nd rnd of last rep of Maze patt. Needle 4: PU 2 sts at top of gusset and 7 (10, 14, 17, 21, 24, 28) sts from side of heel flap, knit rem heel sts.	Cont with needle 1 and dark, PM, work 2nd rnd of last rep of Maze patt for 7 (11, 14, 18, 21, 25, 28) sts. Needle 2: Cont instep in est patt, PM, PU 2 sts at top of gusset, PU 7 (10, 14, 17, 21, 24, 28) sts from side of heel flap, K5 (6, 8, 10, 12, 13, 15) heel sts.
Sts per needle:		
(14, 14, 14), (18, 21, 18), (24, 28, 24), (29, 35, 29), (35, 42, 35), (39, 49, 39), (45, 56, 45)	(14, 7, 7, 14), (18, 14, 7, 18), (24, 14, 14, 24), (29, 21, 14, 29), (35, 21, 21, 35), (39, 28, 21, 39), (45, 28, 28, 45)	(21, 21), (32, 25), (38, 38), (50, 43), (56, 56), (67, 60), (73, 73)

Gusset Decrease

Work first half of sole with dark only. Work 2nd half of sole with dark and light.

4 dpn	5 dpn	2 circular needles
Rnd 1 Needle 1: With dark, work to last 2 sts, ssk. Needle 2: Cont pinstripe patt from instep. Needle 3: Cont pinstripe patt from instep to last 3 sts, K2tog, K1.	**Rnd 1** Needle 1: With dark, work to last 2 sts, ssk. Needles 2 and 3: Cont pinstripe patt from instep. Needle 4: Cont pinstripe patt from instep to last 3 sts, K2tog, K1.	**Rnd 1** Needle 1: With dark, work to last 2 sts before marker, ssk, SM, cont pinstripe patt from instep. Needle 2: Cont pinstripe patt from instep to marker, SM, cont pinstripe patt from instep to last 3 sts, K2tog, K1.
Cont pinstripe patt around foot. When dec for gusset, always work dec st in same yarn, making for a nice patt line on gusset.		
Rnd 2 (dec rnd) Needle 1: Work to last 3 sts, K2tog, K1. Needle 2: Work est patt. Needle 3: K1, ssk, work around.	**Rnd 2 (dec rnd)** Needle 1: Work to last 3 sts, K2tog, K1. Needles 2 and 3: Work est patt. Needle 4: K1, ssk, work around.	**Rnd 2 (dec rnd)** Needle 1: Work to last 3 sts before marker, K2tog, K1, SM, work est patt. Needle 2: Work est patt, SM, K1, ssk, work around.
Rnd 3 Work in Pinstripe patt around. Needle 1: Work est patt. Needle 2: Work est patt. Needle 3: Work est patt.	**Rnd 3** Needle 1: Work est patt. Needles 2 and 3: Work est patt. Needle 4: Work est patt.	**Rnd 3** Needle 1: Work to marker, SM, work est patt. Needle 2: Work est patt to marker, SM, work to end.
Rep rnds 2 and 3 until 28 (44, 56, 72, 84, 100, 112) total sts rem.		

Foot

Cont pinstripe patt to desired heel-to-toe length.	Cont pinstripe patt to desired heel-to-toe length.	Rearrange sts so that all instep sts are on needle 1, and all sole sts are on needle 2. Cont pinstripe patt to desired heel-to-toe length.

Needle 1: Work 1 final row of pinstripe patt. Beg of rnd is at beg of instep; this is needle 1, and sole sts on needles 2 and 3	Needle 1: Work 1 final row of pinstripe patt. Beg of rnd is at beg of instep; this is needle 1, with instep sts on needles 1 and 2 and sole sts on needles 3 and 4.	Needle 1: Instep sts Needle 2: Sole sts
Sts per needle:		
(14, 7, 7), (22, 11, 11), (28, 14, 14), (36, 18, 18), (42, 21, 21), (50, 25, 25), (56, 28, 28)	7 (11, 14, 18, 21, 25, 28)	14 (22, 28, 36, 42, 50, 56)
Toe Shaping		
4 dpn	5 dpn	2 circular needles
Work with dark only.		
Rnd 1 Needle 1: K1, ssk, knit to last 3 sts, K2tog, K1. Needle 2: K1, ssk, knit to end. Needle 3: Knit to last 3 sts, K2tog, K1.	**Rnd 1** Needle 1: K1, ssk, knit to end. Needle 2: Knit to last 3 sts, K2tog, K1. Needle 3: K1, ssk, knit to end. Needle 4: Knit to last 3 sts, K2tog, K1.	**Rnd 1** Needle 1: K1, ssk, knit to last 3 sts, K2tog, K1. Needle 2: K1, ssk, knit to last 3 sts, K2tog, K1.
Rnd 2: Knit around. Rep rnds 1 and 2 until 12 (20, 28, 32, 40, 48, 56) total sts rem. Rep rnd 1 only until 8 (12, 16, 16, 20, 24, 28) total sts rem. Place sts from top of sock on 1 needle and sts from bottom onto 2nd needle. Graft toe sts tog with kitchener st (see page 24).		

Stitch Dictionary

Instructions are for working patterns in the round. Only odd-numbered rounds are shown on charts. On the right-hand side of each chart is a column of white and black squares separated by a blank column. Refer to this first column of squares when working the charts. The basic rule is that on all rows that begin with a white square, you knit the white squares and slip the black squares; on all rows that begin with a black square, you knit the black squares and slip the white squares. Work all even-numbered rows as indicated in the text. On all rounds, work all slip stitches by slipping stitch purlwise with yarn in back.

Caesar's Check

Rnds 1, 5, 9, 13: With B, *K7, (sl 1, K1) 3 times, sl 1, rep from *.

Rnd 2 and all even-numbered rnds: With same color as previous rnd, purl the knit sts worked on previous rnd; sl same slipped sts.

Rnds 3, 7, 11: With A, *K8, (sl 1, K1) 3 times, rep from *.

Rnds 15, 19, 23, 27: With A, * (Sl 1, k1) 3 times, sl 1, K7, rep from *.

Rnds 17, 21, 25: With B, *(K1, sl 1) 3 times, K8, rep from *.

Rnd 28: As rnd 2.

Rep rnds 1–28.

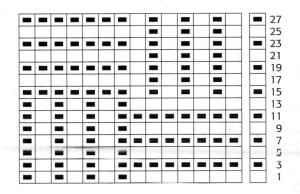

Maze

Rnd 1: With B, *K7, (sl 1, K1) 3 times, sl 1, rep from *.

Rnd 2 and all even-numbered rnds: With same color as previous rnd, knit the knit sts worked on previous rnd; sl same slipped sts.

Rnd 3: With A, *K6, (sl 1, K1) 4 times, rep from *.

Rnd 5: With B, *K5, (sl 1, K1) 4 times, K1, rep from *.

Rnd 7: With A, *K4, (sl 1, K1) 4 times, K2, rep from *.

Rnd 9: With B, *K3, (sl 1, K1) 4 times, K3, rep from *.

Rnd 11: With A, *K2, (sl 1, K1) 4 times, K4, rep from *.

Rnd 13: With B, *(K1, sl 1) 4 times, K6, rep from *.

Rnd 15: With A, *(sl 1, K1) 4 times, K6, rep from *.

Rnd 17: With B, *K1, sl 1, K6, (K1, sl 1) 3 times, rep from *.

Rnd 19: With A, *sl 1, K7, (sl 1, K1) 3 times, rep from *.

Rnd 21: With B, *K1, sl 1, K7, (sl 1, K1) twice, sl 1, rep from *.

Rnd 23: With A, *(sl 1, K1) twice, K6, (sl 1, K1) twice, rep from *.

Rnd 25: With B, *(K1, sl 1) twice, K6, (K1, sl 1) twice, rep from *.

Rnd 27: With A, *(sl 1, K1) 3 times, K6, sl 1, K1, rep from *.

Rnd 29: With B, *(K1, sl 1) 3 times, K7, sl 1, rep from *.

Rnd 31: With A, *(sl 1, K1) 4 times, K6, rep from *.

Rnd 32: As rnd 2.

Rep rnds 1–32.

Crusader's Check

Rnd 1: With B, knit.

Rnd 2 and all even-numbered rnds: With same color as previous rnd, knit (or purl) same sts worked on previous rnd; sl same slipped sts.

Rnd 3: With A, *K2, sl 1, K4, (sl 1, K1) 3 times, sl 1, rep from *.

Rnd 5: With B, *K10, sl 1, K3, rep from *.

Rnd 7: With A, *(K3, sl 1) twice, K5, K1, rep from *.

Rnd 9: With B, *K10, sl 1, K3, rep from *.

Rnd 11: With A, *K4, sl 1, K2, (sl 1, K1) 3 times, sl 1, rep from *.

Rnd 13: With B, knit.

Rnd 15: With A, *(sl 1, K1) 3 times, sl 1, K4, sl 1, K2, rep from *.

Rnd 17: With B, *K3, sl 1, K10, rep from *.

Rnd 19: With A, *sl 1, K5, (sl 1, K3) twice, rep from *.

Rnd 21: With B, *K3, sl 1, K10, rep from *.

Rnd 23: With A, *(sl 1, K1) 3 times, sl 1, K2, sl 1, K4, rep from *.

Rnd 24: As rnd 2.

Rep rnds 1–24.

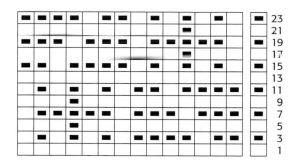

Pharaoh's Check

Rnd 1: With B, knit.

Rnd 2 and all even-numbered rnds: With same color as previous rnd, knit (or purl) same sts worked on previous rnd; sl same slipped sts.

Rnd 3: With A, *(sl 1, K2) twice, sl 1, K7, rep from *.

Rnd 5: With B, *K1, sl 1, K3, sl 1, K8, rep from *.

Rnd 7: With A, *(sl 1, K1) 3 times, sl 1, K7, rep from *.

Rnd 9: With B, *K1, sl 1, K3, sl 1, K8, rep from *.

Rnd 11: With A, *(sl 1, K2) twice, sl 1, K7, rep from *.

Rnd 13: With B, knit.

Rnd 15: With A, *K7, sl 1, (K2, sl 1) twice, rep from *.

Rnd 17: With B, *K8, sl 1, K3, sl 1, K1, rep from *.

Rnd 19: With A, *K7, (sl 1, K1), sl 1, rep from *.

Rnd 21: With B, *K8, sl 1, K3, sl 1, K1, rep from *.

Rnd 23: With A, *K7, sl 1, (K2, sl 1) twice, rep from *.

Rnd 24: As rnd 2.

Rep rnds 1–24.

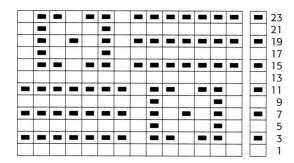

Spearhead

Rnd 1: With B, *K3, sl 1, K5, sl 1, K4, rep from *.

Rnd 2 and all even-numbered rnds: With same color as previous rnd, knit (or purl) same sts worked on previous rnd; sl same slipped sts.

Rnd 3: With A, *sl 1, K1, sl 1, K2, sl 1, K1, sl 1, K2, sl 1, K1, sl 1, rep from *.

Rnd 5: With B, *K4, sl 1, K3, sl 1, K5, rep from *.

Rnd 7: With A, *(K1, sl 1) twice, K5, (sl 1, K1) twice, sl 1, rep from *.

Rnd 9: With B, *K4, (sl 1, K1) 3 times, K4, rep from *.

Rnd 11: With A, *K1, sl 1, K9, sl 1, K1, sl 1, rep from *.

Rnd 13: With B, *K2, (sl 1, K1) 5 times, K2, rep from *.

Rnd 14: As rnd 2.

Rep rnds 1–14.

Double Spiral

Rnd 1: With B, knit.

Rnd 2 and all even-numbered rnds: With same color as previous rnd, knit (or purl) same sts worked on previous rnd; sl same slipped sts.

Rnd 3: With A, *(K1, sl 1) twice, K5, (sl 1, K1) twice, sl 1, rep from *.

Rnd 5: With B, *K4, sl 1, K3, sl 1, K5, rep from * around.

Rnd 7: With A, *K1, sl 1, K3, sl 1, K1, sl 1, K3, sl 1, K1, sl 1, rep from *.

Rnd 9: With B, *K1, (sl 1, K3) 3 times, rep from *.

Rnd 11: With A, *K1, (sl 1, K3) 3 times, K1, rep from *.

Rnd 13: With B, *K4, (sl 1, K3) twice, K1, sl 1, rep from *.

Rnd 15: With A, *(K3, sl 1) 3 times, K2, rep from *.

Rnd 17: With B, *(sl 1, K1) twice, K2, (sl 1, K1) twice, K2, sl 1, K1, rep from *.

Rnd 19: With A, *K5, sl 1, K3, sl 1, K4, rep from *.

Rnd 21: With B, *(sl 1, K1) 3 times, K4, (sl 1, K1) twice, rep from *.

Rnd 23: With A, *knit.

Rnd 25: With B, *(K1, sl 1) twice, K5, (sl 1, K1) twice, sl 1, rep from *.

Rnd 27: With A, *K4, sl 1, K3, sl 1, K5, rep from *.

Rnd 29: With B, *K1, sl 1, K3, (sl 1, K1) twice, K2, sl 1, K1, sl 1, rep from *.

Rnd 31: With A, *K2, (sl 1, K3) 3 times, rep from *.

Rnd 33: With B, *sl 2, K3, sl 1, K3, sl 1, K4, rep from *.

Rnd 35: With A, *K4, (sl 1, K3) twice, K2, rep from *.

Rnd 37: With B, *(K3, sl 1) 3 times, K2, rep from *.

Rnd 39: With A, *sl 1, K1, sl 1, K3, sl 1, K1, sl 1, K3, sl 1, K1, rep from *.

Rnd 41: With B, *K5, sl 1, K3, sl 1, K4, rep from *.

Rnd 43: With A, *(sl 1, K1) twice, sl 1, K5, (sl 1, K1) twice, rep from *.

Rnd 44: As rnd 2.

Rep rnds 1–44.

Bibliography

Bordhi, Cat. *Socks Soar on Two Circular Needles. A Manual of Elegant Knitting Techniques and Patterns.* Friday Harbor, WA: Passing Paws Press, 2001.

Bush, Nancy. *Folk Socks: The History and Techniques of Handknitting Footwear.* Loveland, CO: Interweave Press, 1994.

The Harmony Guide to Knitting Stitches. London: Lyric Books Limited, 1983.

McGregor, Sheila. *The Complete Book of Traditional Scandinavian Knitting.* New York: St. Martin's Press, 1984.

Stanfield, Lesley. *The New Knitting Stitch Library.* Radnor, PA: Chilton Book Company, 1992.

Stanley, Montse. *Reader's Digest Knitter's Handbook.* Pleasantville, NY: Reader's Digest, 1993 (1986).

Thomas, Mary. *Mary Thomas's Book of Knitting Patterns.* New York: Dover, 1972.

Walker, Barbara G. *Charted Knitting Designs: A Third Treasury of Knitting Patterns.* New York: Charles Scribner's Sons, 1972.

———. *A Second Treasury of Knitting Patterns.* New York: Charles Scribner's Sons, 1970.

———. *A Treasury of Knitting Patterns.* New York: Charles Scribner's Sons, 1968.

Wiseman, Nancie M. *The Knitter's Book of Finishing Techniques.* Woodinville, WA: Martingale & Company, 2002.

Yarn Sources

Baby Ull
Dale of Norway Yarn
N16 W23390 Stoneridge Dr., Suite A
Waukesha, WI 53188
www.daleyarns.com

Bearfoot
Weaver's Wool Quarters
Mountain Colors Yarns
PO Box 156
Corvallis, MT 59828
www.mountaincolors.com

Froehlich Special Blauband
Knitter's Underground
308 S. Pennsylvania Ave.
Centre Hall, PA 16828
www.knitters-underground.com

Gems Opal
Louet Sales
808 Commerce Park Dr.
Ogdensburg, NY 13669
www.louet.com/index2.htm

Gjestal Silja Sock Yarn
Plymouth Yarn Company
PO Box 28
Bristol, PA 19007
www.plymouthyarn.com

Kid Mohair & Polwarth
Rovings
Box 28, GRP30 RR#1
Dugald, MB
Canada R0E 0K0
www.rovings.com

Kroy Socks
Patons Yarns
320 Livingstone Ave. S.
Listowel, ON
Canada N4W 3H3
www.patonsyarns.com

Lang JaWoll
Berroco Inc.
14 Elmdale Rd.
Uxbridge, MA 01569
www.berroco.com

Magic Stripes
Lion Brand Yarn
135 Kero Rd.
Carlstadt, NJ 07072
www.lionbrand.com

Meilenweit Fun and Stripes from Lana Grossa
Unicorn Books and Crafts Inc.
1338 Ross St.
Petaluma, CA 95954
www.unicornbooks.com

Regia Plus Cotton Color
Knitting Fever Inc. and Euro Yarns
315 Bayview Ave.
Amityville, NY 11701
www.knittingfever.com

Shepherd Sock
Lorna's Laces
4229 North Honore St.
Chicago, IL 60613
www.lornaslaces.net

Charlene Schurch is the author of several books and numerous articles about knitting. Her articles have appeared in *PieceWork, Spin-Off, Knitter's Magazine,* and *Interweave Knits.* Charlene teaches knitting and dyeing nationally and lives in Florida and Connecticut with her husband, Fred, and cat, Lucy.